Mother Courage
and her Children

Bertolt Brecht was born in Augsburg on 10 February 1898 and died in Berlin on 14 August 1956. He grew to maturity as a playwright in the frenetic years of the twenties and early thirties, with such plays as *Man equals Man*, *The Threepenny Opera* and *The Mother*. He left Germany when Hitler came to power in 1933, eventually reaching the United States in 1941, where he remained until 1947. It was during this period of exile that such masterpieces as *Life of Galileo*, *Mother Courage and her Children* and *The Caucasian Chalk Circle* were written. Shortly after his return to Europe in 1947, he founded the Berliner Ensemble, and from then until his death was mainly occupied in producing his own plays.

Tony Kushner was born in New York City in 1956 and raised in Lake Charles, Louisiana. He is best known for his two-part epic, *Angels in America: A Gay Fantasia on National Themes*. His other plays include: *A Bright Room Called Day*, *Slavs!*, *Hydrotaphia*, *Homebody/Kabul* and the musical *Caroline or Change* for which he wrote book and lyrics, with music by composer Jeanine Tesori. In addition to *Mother Courage and her Children*, Kushner has translated *The Good Person of Sezuan*, Pierre Corneille's *The Illusion*, S.Y. Ansky's *The Dybbuk* and the English-language libretto for the children's opera *Brundibár* by Hans Krasa. He wrote the screenplays for Mike Nichols' film of *Angels in America*, and Steven Spielberg's *Munich*. Tony Kushner is the recipient of a Pulitzer Prize for Drama, an Emmy Award, two Tony Awards, three Obie Awards, an Oscar nomination and an Arts Award from the American Academy of Arts and Letters, among many others. Most recently, *Caroline or Change* received the *Evening Standard* Award, the London Drama Critics' Circle Award and the Olivier Award for Best Musical.

Bertolt Brecht

Mother Courage and her Children

A Chronicle of the Thirty Years' War

Translated by Tony Kushner

Original work entitled
Mutter Courage und ihre Kinder

B L O O M S B U R Y
LONDON • NEW DELHI • NEW YORK • SYDNEY

Bloomsbury Methuen Drama
An imprint of Bloomsbury Publishing Plc

50 Bedford Square	1385 Broadway
London	New York
WC1B 3DP	NY 10018
UK	USA

www.bloomsbury.com

Bloomsbury is a registered trademark of Bloomsbury Publishing Plc

First published 2009
Reprinted 2009, 2011 (twice), 2012 (twice), 2013 (twice), 2014

Original work entitled *Mutter Courage und ihre Kinder* ©
Bertolt-Brecht-Erben/Suhrkamp Verlag 1949
© Bertolt-Brecht-Erben

British Library Cataloguing-in-Publication Data
A catalogue record for this book is available from the British Library.

ISBN: PB: 978-1-4081-2575-5

Library of Congress Cataloging-in-Publication Data
A catalog record for this book is available from the Library of Congress.

Typeset by Country Setting, Kingsdown, Kent
Printed and bound in India

Introduction

Is *Mother Courage and her Children* an anti-war play? It's certainly not a wildly enthusiastic endorsement of war, not a *pro*-war play. Brecht had been an ambulance driver during the First World War, an experience that cured him of any appetite for military conflict. The Thirty Years' War, the setting for *Mother Courage*, in Brecht's dramatic account, was a pointless, grotesquely protracted, gruesome catastrophe for everyone except the handful of victors among the European aristocracy who profited from it. This is an assessment of the conflict to which no historian I've encountered would take exception. War, for Brecht, as it was for the American Civil War General William Tecumseh Sherman, as it is for Mother Courage by the end of the play, as it is assumed to be by most people who haven't lived through it and known to be by nearly everyone who has, is hell.

Driven into exile by the Third Reich, Brecht began work on *Mother Courage* in Sweden in the summer and fall of 1939; he was writing it when Germany invaded Poland. Ten years later, the play received its German premiere at the Deutsches Theater in Berlin. The refugee playwright in his wanderings had circumnavigated the planet. The city to which he returned, once his home and the arena for his great successes, scandals and remarkable theatrical experiments, was now a wasteland of burnt, rat-infested rubble. The Reich was gone, the Second World War had ended, but the Cold War was heating up. The possibility of atomic annihilation overshadowed an uneasy peace. Brecht wrote:

> Let the final inscription then run
> (That broken slab without readers):
> The planet is going to burst.
> Those it bred will destroy it.
> As a way of living together we merely thought up Capitalism.
> Thinking of physics, we thought up rather more:
> A way of dying together.   (*translated by John Willett*)

In 1949, *Mother Courage*'s characters, creator, cast and audience shared a war-weariness and an ashen, heartsick terror at the prospect of more war. It was manifestly one of Brecht's ambitions for the play to expose the transactional, economic nature of war. But by the end of *Mother Courage*, arguably the bleakest conclusion Brecht wrote, his adage that war is business carried on by other means feels inadequate and hollow. The play reveals war not as business but as apocalypse, as the human nemesis, the human antithesis. War devours life.

It's understandable that the play has often been labelled as anti-war, both by those for whom this constitutes high praise and by those for whom *Mother Courage* is evidence that Brecht, writing an ostensibly pacifist text in 1939, supported the Hitler–Stalin non-aggression treaty, thereby unmasking himself as a dull Stalinist drone and obedient functionary of the Comintern.

Emblazoned on the house curtain of the Berliner Ensemble, whose signature production was *Mother Courage*, was a peace dove drawn by Picasso. In a poem about those curtains, Brecht admiringly describes Picasso's peace dove as *streitbare* – 'argumentative' or 'cantankerous' If there's a pacifist, anti-war spirit stirring within *Mother Courage*, it too must be described as *streitbare*, to say the least. It's a problematic sort of anti-war play, given that its climactic, least ambiguous and most hopeful moment is the one in which a town of sleeping people are awakened and summoned to battle against a merciless foe. The great moment of heroism and sacrifice in *Mother Courage*, the great instance of a refusal of obedience to an evil order, is not a refusal to fight but rather a call to arms.

So is that an anti-war play?

Almost all of us believe that war is ghastly and ought to be avoided whenever possible. Most of us don't believe war is always avoidable, but if we've survived it, or tried imaginatively to comprehend its horrors, we dread its outbreak. Non-violence isn't a course most of us can embrace, but its arguments, if not persuasive, are compelling to any thoughtful person: there's very little evidence in history that war brings peace. There's ample evidence that, given our assumption of war's inevitability, we're more than a little susceptible to militarist advocacy for wholehearted and constant preparedness and, when our troops are engaged in combat, for a blinders-on determination to win. In other words, pacifists and militarists and the vast rest of us in between, have contradictory thoughts and feelings about war, even to the point of torment. Simple plays with simple, single answers can be of little use to us.

Bertolt Brecht was not a simple man. His personality and his politics are fascinatingly complex, as is his theoretical writing, his poetry, his plays, all of which are remarkably resistant to reductive labeling. *Mother Courage and her Children*, in my opinion the greatest of his many great works, is not a simple play. It places us in judgement of the actions of a woman who inhabits a universe defined by war, who often makes calamitous choices but who makes them faced with scarcities and perils so severe that her choices are unbearably hard, and sometimes all but impossible. She refuses to understand the nature of her tragic circumstances; she refuses to look back; she is afraid looking back will weaken her. She reaches correct conclusions and then immediately discards them. She's afraid she can't afford to learn. She presents us with a maddening and dismaying spectacle; she refuses to judge herself, and we judge her for that. And also, we watch her world grow lonelier and less forgiving with each bad choice she makes. We feel we are watching her dying – the losses she countenances would kill anyone – yet she refuses to die. We judge even that refusal; her indomitability, her hardiness, come to seem dehumanising, uncanny, less mythic than monstrous.

And yet we are moved by this woman, as, inarguably, Brecht meant us to be. She's egoistical because she has almost nothing. She's selfish but she's spared nothing. She has a vitality and a carnality. Even though her appetites seem obscene, set as they are against widespread carnage, the mortification of Courage's dignity, of her flesh, the grinding-down of her ambition and self-possession, are devastating to watch. She's smart and she thinks her cleverness has gained her the little something, the small sufficiency – her wagon – by means of which she attains a degree of agency and power in her malevolent, anti-human world. The shattering of that illusion of power leads her to self-loathing and from that to a bitter contempt for the powerless, and then on to a creeping slow stupidity, leaving us with a terrible sense of loss.

The smartass, sceptical, secular intelligence governing *Courage* is at war with a fatal darkness that suffuses the action. As with nearly all of Brecht's big plays written in exile, *Courage* is set at one of the many transitional historical moments when the medieval is yielding to the mercantile (a process arguably still incomplete). The bad new things are preferable, according to another of Brecht's adages, to the good old things, but in *Courage*, a pre-modern, peasant Christianity is set against the onslaught of the modern, the vehicle for which is the war. It's impossible to resist the power of this sorrowful Christian ethos of redemptive suffering. It is equally impossible to imagine for it any existence in the Hobbesian war-of-all-against-all world of *Mother Courage* – our world – other than as the nearly subliminal, nearly sublingual, poetic, oppositional spectre that haunts and at a few critical moments possesses Brecht's play, which at least in part accounts for its divided pro- and anti-war soul.

In her blindness to the Pyrrhic nature of her victories each time she succeeds in hanging on to the goods she sells, Courage embodies an uncomfortably familiar modern disfigurement: a relationship to commodities, to money and the marketplace, to the non-human and the inorganic that perverts human relationships and is ultimately inimical to life. And yet . . . what else can she do? If she's oblivious to the consequences of hanging on, she's eagle-eyed about the consequences of losing what she has. Neither Courage nor Kattrin will have to sell herself – neither will end up like the prostitute Yvette – as long as they've got boots, buckles, beer and black-market bullets to sell instead. Courage isn't neglecting any plausible, palatable, even endurable alternative. In choosing to write about a canteen woman trailing after armies in war-ravaged seventeenth-century Europe, Brecht precluded any alternatives or options from presenting themselves. If his formal inventions – the jarring succession of bluntly spliced juxtapositions and epic theatrical chronological elisions and leaps, the probing of the social basis of character, of personality – invite us to adopt a stance of critical observation, his choices of time and place and circumstance force us out of judgement and into empathy.

There's a life in *Courage*'s details that refuses to participate in anything schematic. Like all great plays, *Courage* instructs; and its instruction flashes forth from within a churning, disorienting action, compounded of conflict, of contradiction. Clarity is intended, but confusion is no accident. What *Courage* shows us will escape our judgement, but it remains infinitely available to our arguments, to our struggles to understand.

Tony Kushner, August 2009

Mother Courage
and her Children

This translation of *Mother Courage and her Children* was commissioned by the Public Theater, New York (Oskar Eustis, Artistic Director), and first presented on 21 August 2006 at the Public's Delacorte Theater in Central Park, directed by George C. Wolfe, with a score by Jeanine Tesori. The sets were designed by Riccardo Hernandez, costumes by Marina Draghici, lights by Paul Gallo and sound by Acme Sound Partners. The cast, in alphabetical order, was as follows:

The Colonel/Older Soldier/ Injured Farmer	Raul Aranas
Swiss Cheese	Geoffrey Arend
Quartermaster/ Soldier with Fur Coat	Max Baker
Young Soldier/Lieutenant	Ato Essandoh
Old Woman/Voice Inside	Colleen Fitzpatrick
Army Recruiter/Soldier	Glenn Fleshler
The One with the Eyepatch/ Soldier	Michael Izquierdo
Soldier	Eugene Jones
Cook	Kevin Kline
Sergeant	George Kmeck
Yvette Pottiers	Jenifer Lewis
Clerk/Soldier	Paco Lozano
Soldier	Michael Markham
General/Farmer	Larry Marshall
Young Man with Mattress/ First Soldier	Jack Noseworthy
The Chaplain	Austin Pendleton
Soldier	Sean Phillips
Farmer's Son	Silvestre Rasuk
Mother Courage	Meryl Streep
Kattrin	Alexandra Wailes
Eilif	Frederick Weller
Injured Farmer's Wife/ Farmer's Wife	Jade Wu
Sergeant/ Regimental Secretary	Waleed F. Zuaiter

Mother Courage and her Children in this translation had its first British production in the Olivier auditorium of the National Theatre, London, on 9 September 2009. The cast, in alphabetical order, was as follows:

The One with the Eyepatch	Anthony Mark Barrow
Soldier	William J. Cassidy
The Regimental Secretary	Johannes Flaschberger
The Chaplain	Peter Gowen
The Clerk	Jonathan Gunthorpe
The Sergeant	Stephen Kennedy
The Quartermaster	Youssef Kerkour
The Cook	Martin Marquez
Young Soldier	Louis McKenzie
Farmer's Son	Kyle McPhail
Farmer's Wife	Siobhán McSweeney
Swiss Cheese	Harry Melling
Farmer's Wife	Eleanor Montgomery
Older Soldier	Stephen O'Toole
Yvette	Charlotte Randle
Soldier	Guy Rhys
Eilif	Clifford Samuel
The Sergeant	Gary Sefton
Mother Courage	Fiona Shaw
The Colonel/The Lieutenant	Roger Sloman
The General	Colin Stinton
Kattrin	Sophie Stone
Young Man	Morgan Watkins
The Army Recruiter	Sargon Yelda

Other parts played by members of the Company

Director Deborah Warner
Set Designer Tom Pye
Associate Designer Vicki Fifield
Costume Designer Ruth Myers
Lighting Designer Jean Kalman
Songs Duke Special
Video Designers Lysander Ashton and Mark Grimmer
Sound Designers Andrew Bruce and Nick Lidster

Characters

Mother Courage
Kattrin, *her mute daughter*
Eilif, *her oldest son*
Swiss Cheese, *her youngest son*
The Sergeant *in Scene One*
The Army Recruiter
The Cook
The General
The Chaplain
The Quartermaster
Yvette Pottier
The One with the Eyepatch
The Colonel
The Sergeant *in Scene Three*
The Clerk
The Young Soldier
The Older Soldier
The Farmer *in Scene Five*
The Farmer's Wife *in Scene Five*
The Regimental Secretary
The Old Woman
The Young Man
The Voice Inside
The Lieutenant
The Farmer *in Scene Eleven*
The Farmer's Wife *in Scene Eleven*
The Farmer's Son
Soldiers

One

A road outside of town.

A **Sergeant** *and an* **Army Recruiter** *stand waiting, shivering.*

The Army Recruiter   How's a recruiter going to find
recruits in a place like this? Orders from the General Staff,
four fresh companies in two weeks time! I contemplate suicide,
Sergeant. And the people here are so lacking in fundamental
decency they've given me insomnia! Imagine if you will some
jerk, concave chest, veiny legs, a total zero. I buy him beers till
he's shitfaced, he signs up, and then: I'm paying the tab, he's
off to take a leak, he says, I try to keep an eye on him because
I've learned the smell of rat, and sure enough, zzzzzzzip!
Jump up and fled like a louse flees louse-powder. A handshake's
meaningless, honour and duty are empty words. A place like
this, you lose your conviction in the Inner Goodness of Man,
Sergeant.

The Sergeant   The problem with these people is they
haven't had enough war. Where else do morals come from?
War! Everything rots in peacetime. People turn into carefree
rutting animals and nobody fucking cares. Everyone overeats,
whatever they want, 'Oh I'll just sit down now and eat a big
cheese and fatback sandwich on fluffy white bread.' Think
these people know how many young men and horses they've
got? Why count? It's peacetime! I've been in some towns
that've gone seventy years without any war whatsoever, people
hadn't even bothered naming their children, no one knew
whose was whose. You need a bit of butchery to get them
counting and listing and naming: big piles of empty boots,
corn bagged for portage, man and cow alike stamped and
mobilised. War makes order, order makes war.

The Army Recruiter   Amen.

The Sergeant   It isn't easy, starting a war, but nothing worthwhile is easy. And once you're in, you're hooked like a gambler, you can't afford to walk away from the crapshoot once you're deep into it. You become as afraid of peace as you ever were of war, no one really wants the fighting to end. You just have to get people used to the idea. Everyone's scared of anything changing.

The Army Recruiter   Heads up, a wagon. Two boys appropriate age. Tell 'em to pull over. If this goes bust I'm packing it in, I'm kissing the April wind goodbye.

A Jew's harp offstage. A canteen wagon comes down the road. It's pulled by two young men, **Eilif** *and* **Swiss Cheese**. *In the wagon, driving it,* **Mother Courage***; seated besides her, playing the Jew's harp, her mute daughter* **Kattrin**.

Mother Courage   Morning, Sergeant.

The **Sergeant** *blocks the wagon.*

The Sergeant   Morning, people. Declare yourselves!

Mother Courage   Retail!

She sings:

> To feed a war you have to pillage,
> But let your soldiers rest a bit:
> For what they need, here's Mother Courage,
> With woolen coats and boots that fit!
> Their heads ablaze with lice and liquor,
> The boys are marching to the beat!
> I guarantee they'll step it quicker
> With boots upon their blistered feet!

Mother Courage and her Sons (*singing*)
> Now Spring has come, and Winter's dead.
> The snow has gone, so draw a breath!
> Let Christian souls crawl out of bed,
> Pull on their socks and conquer death!

Mother Courage (*singing*)
Unless his belly's full of porridge,
A soldier's sure to turn and run.
Buy him some grub from Mother Courage –
So he'll know where to point his gun.
They fight for God and legal tender,
I'll see them clothed, and feed them well,
And bless the boys, in all their splendour,
As they march down the road to hell.

Mother Courage and her Sons (*singing*)
Now Spring has come, and Winter's dead.
The snow has gone, so draw a breath!
Let Christian souls crawl out of bed,
Pull on their socks and conquer death!

The wagon starts to roll again. Again the **Sergeant** *blocks it.*

The Sergeant   Hang on a minute, garbage. What's your regiment?

Eilif   Second Finnish.

The Sergeant   Paperwork!

Mother Courage   Paperwork?

Swiss Cheese   She's Mother Courage.

The Sergeant   I never heard of her. Why's she called 'Courage'?

Mother Courage   They called me Courage because I was scared of financial ruin, Sergeant, so I drove my wagon straight through the cannon fire at Riga, with fifty loaves of bread turning mouldy – I didn't see that I had a choice.

The Sergeant   Fascinating, now I know your life's story, gimme your paperwork.

Mother Courage *reaches behind her, finds a battered tin box, removes a big stack of tattered paper. She climbs down off the wagon.*

Mother Courage   Here's paper, all I possess. A prayer book I bought in Alt-Ötting, I use the pages to wrap pickles, and a map of Moravia, will I ever get to Moravia? God knows. If I don't the map's for the cat to shit on. And here, official proof my horse doesn't have hoof-and-mouth disease, which is swell except the horse is dead, poor thing, fifteen guilders she cost, although praise Jesus, not *my* fifteen guilders. I have more paper if you want it.

The Sergeant   What I want is, I want your licence to sell. You want my boot up your ass?

Mother Courage   Excuse me but you may not discuss my ass in front of my children, that's disgusting. And my ass is not for you. The Second Finnish Regiment never required any licence besides my patent honesty which, if you had a better character, you could read off my face.

The Army Recruiter   Sergeant, I think this woman's insubordinate. The King's army needs discipline.

Mother Courage   And sausages!

The Sergeant   Name.

Mother Courage   Anna Fierling.

The Sergeant   And these others are Fierlings?

Mother Courage   Who? I'm Fierling. Not them.

The Sergeant   They're your children.

Mother Courage   They are. What's your problem? (*Pointing to her elder son.*) Take him for example, he's Finnish, he's Eilif Nojocki, why? His father was Kojocki or Mojocki so I split the difference. The boy's got fond memories of his father, only it's not actually his father he remembers but a French guy with a goatee. Regardless, he inherited the Kojocki or Mojocki brains; that man could steal a farmer's socks without removing the boots first. None of us has the same name.

The Sergeant   None of you?

Mother Courage   Four points on the compass and I've been pricked in every direction.

The Sergeant (*pointing at the youngest son*)   I bet. Was his father Chinese?

Mother Courage   Bad guess. Swiss.

The Sergeant   He came along after the French guy?

Mother Courage   French guy? I never knew any French guys, try to follow or we'll be here till night falls. His father was Swiss, as in Switzerland, but *his* name's Fejos because he's not named after his father, who built fortresses, drunk.

Swiss Cheese *smiles proudly, nodding.* **Kattrin** *hides a laugh.*

The Sergeant   Then who was Fejos?

Mother Courage   I don't mean to be rude, but you're entirely devoid of imagination, aren't you? I more or less had to call him Fejos because when he came out I was with a Hungarian. He couldn't care less, the Hungarian, he was dying, his kidneys shrivelled up even though he was abstemious. A nice man, the boy looks just like him.

The Sergeant   But he wasn't the father.

Mother Courage   Nevertheless. His big talent is pulling the wagon, so I call him Swiss Cheese. (*Pointing to her daughter.*) She's Kattrin Haupt. Half-German.

The Sergeant   Jesus. A nice wholesome family.

Mother Courage   We are. I've crossed the wide world in this wagon.

The Sergeant   You're Bavarian. I'm guessing Bamberg. What're you doing in Sweden?

Mother Courage   There's no war in Bamberg, is there? Was I supposed to wait?

The Army Recruiter   So, Jacob and Esau Ox. Does she ever unstrap the rig and turn you loose to graze?

Eilif   Mama, can I punch this asshole in the mouth? Please?

Mother Courage   Can you stay where you are and keep quiet, please? Now, Officers, how's about a good pistol, or a belt buckle? Sergeant, your buckle's all bent.

The Sergeant   How's about you tell me instead why these two boys who are solid as birch trees with chests and legs like Arabian chargers aren't in the army.

Mother Courage (*quick*)   Drop it, Sergeant, my kids aren't suited for war work.

The Army Recruiter   They look suitable to me. Make a little money, get famous. Selling shoes, that's for women. (*To* **Eilif**.) Come here. You talk big. But maybe you're a chicken.

Mother Courage   He is. He's a chicken. Look at him cross-eyed, he'll faint.

The Army Recruiter   I'm crossing my eyes, he still looks good to me!

The **Army Recruiter** *gestures to* **Eilif** *to follow him.*

Mother Courage   He's mine, not yours.

The Army Recruiter   He called me an asshole. I invite him to accompany me to the field over there so I can clobber him.

Eilif   Glad to. Don't fret, Mama, I'll be right back.

Mother Courage   Don't you move, you brawling lump! (*To the* **Army Recruiter**, *pointing at* **Eilif**.) Watch out, he's got a knife sheathed in his boot!

The Army Recruiter   A knife, huh? I'll extract it easy as a baby tooth. This way, baby boy.

Mother Courage (*to the* **Sergeant**)   You listen to me, your Captain has been ogling my daughter, and I'm going to tell him you're making her unhappy and he'll clap you in the stocks.

The Sergeant (*to the* **Army Recruiter**)   No fighting, OK? (*To* **Mother Courage**.) What's so terrible about a job in the army? Bet his daddy was a soldier! Died a hero or something?

Mother Courage   Or something, dead at any rate, and (*pointing at* **Eilif**) he's just a child! I know your kind, you'll get a five-guilder fee and he'll get slaughtered!

The Army Recruiter   We'll give him a soldier's snazzy hat and brand new regulation boots when he signs.

Eilif   I don't want you to give me shit.

Mother Courage   Hey hey hey, I got a fun idea, let's you and me go fishing said the fisherman to the worm. (*To* **Swiss Cheese**.) Run tell the Captain they're stealing your brother!

She pulls a knife.

He's mine! He's not going to war! I'll poke your eyes out first, you cannibals. We're merchants, we sell ham and shirts and we're friendly people.

The Sergeant   Yeah, you look friendly. Put up the knife, you old cunt. If there's a war, there have to be soldiers, right?

Mother Courage   Somebody else's kids, not mine.

The Sergeant   And there it is, your brood gets fat off the war but you think it's a one-way transaction. Maybe your sons have courage even if you don't.

Eilif   The war doesn't scare me.

The Sergeant   Why would it? See any bruises on me? I joined at seventeen!

Mother Courage   Let's see how close you get to seventy.

The Sergeant   What're you insinuating? I'm gonna get killed?

Mother Courage   You look marked to me. What if you're just a cadaver who hasn't heard the bad news, hmm?

Swiss Cheese   She can see things, everyone knows that, she sees into the future.

The Army Recruiter   Tell the Sergeant his future then. He likes a good laugh.

The Sergeant   That's crap. Seeing things.

Mother Courage   Give me your helmet.

He does.

The Sergeant   Whatever you're doing, it means as much as dried turds in dead grass.

Mother Courage *looks at him, asking if she should continue.*

The Sergeant   Go ahead, it'll make a good story

She tears a piece of paper in two.

Mother Courage   Eilif, Swiss Cheese, Kattrin, we'll all be torn to scrap like this, if we let the war pull us in too deeply. (*To the* **Sergeant**.) For a friend I do it for free. I make a black cross on the paper. Black is death.

Swiss Cheese   And see the other piece of paper's empty.

Mother Courage   I fold them, I tumble 'em together, topsy turvy as we all tumble together, the marked and unremarkable, from mother love onward, and now draw and now you'll know.

The **Sergeant** *hesitates.*

The Army Recruiter (*to* **Eilif**)   I'm the pickiest recruiter in the Swedish Army, most don't come close to making the cut but maybe you've got the grit, the beans, that special fire.

The **Sergeant** *reaches in the helmet.*

The Sergeant   It's all gobbledegook, oooh, the scales are falling from my eyes!

He draws a piece of paper, unfolds it.

Swiss Cheese   Uh-oh! The black cross! He's going away!

The Army Recruiter   There are more soldiers than bullets. Don't let them scare you.

The Sergeant (*hoarse*)   You cheated me.

Mother Courage   You did that to yourself the day you enlisted. Now we'll get going, it isn't every day there's a war on, we don't want to miss out on the fun.

The Sergeant   Hell and the Devil, you cheated me, bitch, but you'll be sorry you did! Your bastard's a soldier now!

Eilif   I wanna go with them, Mama.

Mother Courage   Shut your mouth, nasty!

Eilif   Swiss Cheese too, he wants to be a soldier too!

Mother Courage   You think so? Says who? Draw your own papers from the helmet, all three of you, then we'll see what's what.

She goes behind the wagon, where she tears paper and marks slips with crosses.

The Army Recruiter (*to* **Eilif**)   And I've heard the enemy propaganda, in the Swedish Army it's Bible study and hymn singing night and day, but between us, the army's the army and once you're in you're washed clean of sin, and you can sing any song you like.

Mother Courage *returns with the helmet.*

Mother Courage   Time to abandon mother, huh, my two terrors? War is irresistible to young knuckleheads like you. Draw, draw and see what a welcome the world has in store. You bet I'm terrified, Sergeant, you would be too if you'd given birth to 'em, each one has a horrible personality defect. (*To Eilif.*) Here. Fish out your ticket.

Eilif *picks a slip of paper. She snatches it from him and unfolds it.*

Mother Courage   Oh I'm an unlucky mother! My womb only ever gave me grief after grief after grief! So young, into the army and then rotting in the ground, grass waving over him, it's hideously clear. You see, you see! A cross! Marked! Your father was a brazen idiot, like you, but you learned from me: think or die. Just like the paper shows.

She flattens **Eilif**.

Mother Courage   ARE YOU GOING TO THINK???!!!

Eilif   Sure, why not?

Mother Courage   And if they laugh and call you a chicken just cluck at them, who cares?

The Army Recruiter   If you've crapped your pants we can take your brother instead.

Mother Courage   Cluck! Cluck! Laugh right back! (*To* **Swiss Cheese**.) Now you, Swiss Cheese, fish for it. I'm not much worried about you, honest as you are.

Swiss Cheese *draws a slip from the helmet. He stares at it.*

Mother Courage   It's empty, isn't it? It can't be you pulled a black cross, that I'm losing you too, can't be.

She takes the slip from him.

Mother Courage   A cross! I guess because he's the simple son? Swiss Cheese, you're also going down unless you're always honest, like I taught you when you were a tiny kid – always bring back exact change from the baker. Otherwise you're lost. See, Sergeant, a black cross, yeah?

The Sergeant   Yeah. But I don't get it. I stay back, I never go near the fighting, why'd I get one? (*To the* **Army Recruiter**.) She's not a swindler, even her own kids get marked.

Swiss Cheese   Even I'm marked. But I get it, I'm obedient.

Mother Courage (*to* **Kattrin**)   You're safe, I know it, you won't draw a cross because you are the cross I bear: your good heart.

She holds the helmet up to **Kattrin**, *but she snatches the slip out herself before* **Kattrin** *has a chance.*

Mother Courage   I'm completely desperate. Something's wrong, maybe the way I stirred them. You can't be so kind, Kattrin, not any more, a cross stands athwart the road for you too. Stay quiet always, that should be easy for a mute. So now you all know, safety first, all of you. Back to the wagon and let's get far away from here.

Mother Courage *hands the* **Sergeant** *his helmet and climbs back up on the wagon.*

The Army Recruiter (*to the* **Sergeant**)   Do something!

The Sergeant   I feel funny.

The Army Recruiter   You have to wear your hat in wind like this, now you're getting sick. Catch her up in some haggling. (*Loud.*) At least take a look at the merchandise, Sergeant, these nice people have to make a living, right? Wait a minute, lady, the Sergeant here wants a buckle.

Mother Courage   A half-guilder. Though buckles like mine are worth two guilders easy.

She climbs down from the wagon, pulls out a box of belt buckles.

The Sergeant   It looks like it was chewed on. I'm shivering with this wind, let me look it over back here.

He goes behind the wagon.

Mother Courage   Doesn't seem windy to me.

The Sergeant   A half-guilder, maybe, it's silver.

Mother Courage (*going behind the wagon*)   Solid six ounces.

The Army Recruiter (*to* **Eilif**)   And now let's go get drunk, you and me, man to man, I have a pocket full of change.

Eilif *hesitates, undecided.*

Mother Courage   OK, a half-guilder, done deal.

The Sergeant   I just don't get it. I stay in the rear, I find a safe place, a sergeant's prerogative, I let the others go for the glory. Now I won't manage to keep my lunch down, I can tell, I'm queasy all of a sudden.

Mother Courage   Don't let it ruin your appetite. Here, take a slug of schnapps, man, and stick to the rear.

She gives him a drink. The **Army Recruiter** *has taken* **Eilif**'s *arm and is leading him away.*

The Army Recruiter   Ten guilders up front, and you're a brave warrior for the King, and all the women go for you. And you can punch me in the mouth for insulting you.

They go out. Dumb **Kattrin** *jumps down from the wagon and starts making wild loud noises.*

Mother Courage   Wait Kattrin, wait a minute. The Sergeant's paying.

She bites the half-guilder the **Sergeant**'s *given her.*

I've been burned, Sergeant, never learned to trust money. And now – where's Eilif?

Swiss Cheese   With the recruiter. Gone.

Mother Courage (*stands frozen, then*)   You're simplicity itself, you are. (*To* **Kattrin**.) I know, I know, you can't speak, it isn't your fault.

The Sergeant   Give yourself a little schnapps, Mama. So goes the world. It's not so terrible, a soldier's life.

Mother Courage   You have to help your brother pull, Kattrin.

Side by side, brother and sister harness themselves to the wagon and pull it away. **Mother Courage** *walks alongside. They exit.*

The Sergeant (*watching them leave*)
    If off the war you hope to live,
    Take what you can. You'll also give.

Two

FROM 1625 TO 1626 MOTHER COURAGE FOLLOWS
THE SWEDISH ARMY AS IT CROSSES POLAND. NEAR
THE FORT AT WALLHOF SHE SEES HER SON AGAIN.
THE LUCKY SALE OF A CHICKEN AND A GREAT DAY
FOR THE BRAVE SON.

*The **General**'s tent.*

*Beside the tent, the kitchen. Cannon fire in the distance. The **Cook** argues with **Mother Courage** who hopes to sell him a chicken.*

The Cook   Sixty hellers for that scraggly hen?

Mother Courage   Scraggly? This fat beast? What, your General, who can outeat anyone from Sweden to Poland and back again, and woe unto the cook who serves him up a skimpy table, he can't cough up sixty little hellers?

The Cook   For ten hellers on any street corner I can fetch a dozen birds better looking than that.

Mother Courage   Sure, sure you can get a fat chicken like this on a street corner with everyone from miles about all withered and skeletal. You'll fetch a rat from the fields, maybe, *maybe*, if you can find one, they've all been eaten, I saw five men chase one rat for hours. Fifty hellers for this, this, what would you call it, well it's practically a turkey, it's so big. And in the middle of a siege.

The Cook   We're not in the middle of a siege, it's them up in the fort that are in the middle of the siege, we're the besiegers. Try to keep it straight.

Mother Courage   Why bother, the besiegers have less food than the besieged. They hauled all the crops and cattle up to the fort before they locked themselves in. I hear they're swimming in sauce and beer up there. Down here, well, I've been to the farms. Grim. Zilch.

The Cook   They've got it, the farmers. They hide it.

Mother Courage (*playing her trump*)   They've got nothing, starving, I've seen them, digging roots up out of the ground and sucking their fingers after a meal of boiled leather. And I'm supposed to sell a gourmet capon for forty hellers.

The Cook   I offered thirty, not forty.

Mother Courage   This isn't any workaday chicken. He was musically gifted, he'd eat only to the tune of his favorite marches, and he could do arithmetic. All that for forty hellers? If you don't have something to serve him, your General's liable to eat your head.

The Cook   Know why I'm not worried?

He spears a piece of beef with his knife and lifts it up.

A roast for roasting. I've tendered you my final offer.

Mother Courage   Roast it, but hurry, it's been dead three weeks and it stinks.

The Cook   I saw it running across the fields yesterday.

Mother Courage   Praise Jesus, a dead dog, running around. It's a miracle.

The Cook   It was a cow, not a dog, and after two hours in a stewpot, it'll be tender as a tit.

Mother Courage   After five hours, it'll be glue, but say a prayer if the general comes hungry, and keep the pepper handy, I'm telling you, it stinks.

*The **General**, a **Chaplain** and **Eilif** enter the **General**'s tent. The **General** claps **Eilif**'s shoulder.*

The General   Come on, son, sit at the right hand of your General. You're a hero and a real Christian and this is a war for God and what's done is done because God wants it done and you did it and I feel fantastic! When we take the goddamned fort I'm going to give you a gold bracelet. We come to set their souls free, and what do they do, these farmers who've happily let centuries of their beefsteak disappear down the gullets of fat Polish priests? They decide to turn their livestock loose so we can't eat. Savages. Ingrates. Stinky little shitpeople. But they'll remember what they learned from you, boy!

He pours wine into two tin cups, then offers one to **Eilif***.*

The General   Here's a can of my best red, we'll bolt it down together.

Eilif *and* **General** *gulp down the wine.*

The General   Chaplain can lap up the dregs, like the suffering Christ he is. Now what's for lunch, heart of my hearts?

Eilif   Umm . . . steak!

The General (*screaming to the kitchen*)   Cook! Meat!

The Cook   He knows we're out of everything so he brings guests.

Mother Courage *gestures to him to be silent, so she can hear what's happening in the tent.*

Eilif   You really work up an appetite, butchering peasants.

Mother Courage   Jesus, it's my Eilif.

The Cook   Who?

Mother Courage   My eldest. Haven't laid eyes on him for two years, stolen from me on the open road, and he must be in great good favour with the General, his special lunch guest, and what're you going to feed them, nothing! You heard the General: meat! My advice: buy the chicken. Price: one hundred hellers.

The General   Lunch, Lamb, you beast-who-barely-learned-to-cook, or I'll hook and gut you!

The Cook   Oh hell, give it, it's blackmail.

Mother Courage   This shabby bird?

The Cook   Just give it to me, it's a sin, fifty hellers for scraggle like that.

Mother Courage   I said a hundred, one whole guilder. Nothing's too nice for my eldest, the General's special guest.

*The **Cook** gives her the money.*

The Cook   Plucking included. While I get the fire up.

Mother Courage (*sitting down, plucking*)   The look on his face when he sees it's me! He's my brave, clever boy. I've got another one, stupid but honest. The girl's nothing. At least she's quiet, at least there's that.

*The **General** pours another drink. They keep drinking, getting drunker.*

The General   Have another, son, a lip-smacking Falernian, only one or maybe two kegs left, but I don't begrudge my best for my true believers. Who act! Not like this watery-eyed old simp of a soul-shepherd, he preaches sunup to sundown till the whole church is out cold and snoring but we still haven't taken the goddamned fort and don't ask him how to do it, or how to do anything. You, Eilif, my son, on the other hand, you showed an initiative which eventuated in the requisitioning of twenty head of cattle from some farmers. Which will arrive soon I hope.

Eilif   By morning.

Mother Courage   That's thoughtful of my Eilif, delivering the oxen tomorrow, otherwise I doubt my chicken would've had such an enthusiastic reception.

The General   Regale us!

Eilif   Yep, well, this is the way it went: I heard the farmers were sneaking out at night all hush-hush to round up these cows they were hiding in a woods. They'd arranged a sale of the cows with the people up in the fort. I held back, let the farmers do all the work rounding up the cows – they're good at herding, saved me the work. Meanwhile I got my men good and ready, for two days I fed them only bread and water, so they got crazy for meat, they'd drool if they just heard the word 'meat', if they even heard a word beginning with 'M', like . . . um . . . 'meat'!

The General   You're smart.

Eilif   I dunno. After that it was basically one-two-three. Except the farmers had huge clubs and they outnumbered us three to one and when they saw we wanted their cows they came after us like murder. Four of them got me backed up against a thornbush and one of them clouted the sword from out of my hand and they were hollering 'give up' and I thought right, I give up and you pound me to paste.

The General   What'd you do?

Eilif   I started laughing.

The General   What?

Eilif   I laughed. So then they wanted to discuss that. So I start bargaining: 'You're fucking kidding, twenty guilders for that ox? More like fifteen tops!' Like we're doing business. Which confuses them, they're scratching their heads. And that's when I picked up my cutlass and I cut their heads off, HUH! HUH! HUH! HUH! All four of them. Necessity trumps the commandments. Right?

The General   Want to rule on that, you pious pedant?

The Chaplain   There's no such exemption in the Bible, in the literal sense, but back then Our Lord could take five loaves of bread and make five hundred, so there was no necessity per se. You can command people to love their neighbours and if they're full of bread they may comply. That was then and this is now.

The General (*laughing*)   You can say that again. Here, you need to whet your whistle after that, Pharisee.

He pours the **Chaplain** *a glass of wine.*

The General (*to* **Eilif**)   You massacred the farmers and now my brave boys'll bite down on a bit of real red meat, and how could God gripe about that? Doesn't His Holy Writ say 'Whateversoever thou dost for the least of My brethren is done for Me'? It'll be like in the old days again, a bit of beef, a gulp of wine and then fight for God.

Eilif   I snatched up my sword and I split their skulls in two!

The General   You're a Caesar in the making. You ought to meet His Majesty.

Eilif   I saw him once, distantly. He kind of gives off light. I want to be just like him.

The General   You already are. I treasure you, Eilif, brave soldier boy, you're my own son, that's how I'll handle you.

He leads **Eilif** *to a big map.*

The General   Here's the picture, Eilif, the whole campaign. So much to do.

In the kitchen, **Courage** *stops eavesdropping and resumes plucking the chicken, furious.*

Mother Courage   That's one lousy General.

The Cook   No he's not, he eats to excess but he's good at what he does.

Mother Courage   If he knew what he was doing he wouldn't need brave soldiers, he could make do with ordinary soldiers. It's when the General's a moron the soldiers have to be brave. It's when the King's pinching his pennies and doesn't hire enough soldiers, every soldier has to be hard-working. You only need brave hard-working patriot soldiers when the country's coming unglued. In a decent country that's properly managed with decent kings and generals, people can be just what people are, common and of middling intelligence and for all I care every one of them a shivering coward. In a decent country that's properly managed.

The General   A man like you was born a soldier.

Eilif   My daddy was. A soldier. My mother taught me a song about it.

The General   Sing it for me! (*Hollering.*) Where's my goddam food?!

Eilif   It's called 'The Song about the Soldier and His Wife',

He sings, doing a sabre dance:

'Your gun is precise, and your bayonet's nice –
But the ice on the river won't hold you.
You'll drown in a trice if you march on the ice.
And lonely cold death shall enfold you!'

Thus spoke his wife, as he whetted his knife;
Hoisting his pack he said, 'Marching's my life!
When you're marching no woman can scold you.
When you're marching no woman can scold you.
We're marching into Poland,
Then we're marching off to Spain!
With your bayonet sharpened –
With your sharp bayonet you've no need to explain!
No woman ever controlled you!'

Oh bitter her tears, she was younger in years,
But wiser than he, so she told him.
March off if he must, it will all come to dust –
For only a coffin shall hold him.
Off goes her man, he will write when he can,
And women have wept since the world first began,
And her weeping has often consoled him.
The sound of her sorrow consoled him.

With the moon on the shingles,
Icy white on the snow,
Wave goodbye to your husband!
So long to your husband and then back home you go,
Where you'll wait for the fate you foretold him!

Mother Courage, *in the kitchen, takes up his song, beating time on a pot with spoon.*

Mother Courage (*singing*)
It isn't a joke. Your life is like smoke.
And someday you'll wish you had tarried.
Oh, how quickly you'll fall. Oh God. Help us all.
Soldiers should never get married.

Eilif Who's that?

Mother Courage (*singing*)
>He tumbled the dice and he soon paid the price:
>They gave him his orders to march on the ice.
>And the water rose up all around him.
>And the water rose up and it drowned him.
>Through Poland, through Spain, his poor wife searched
>   in vain.
>But he'd vanished, and she never found him.
>He was gone and his wife never found him.

The General   Who told them they could sing in my kitchen?

Eilif *goes into the kitchen. He sees his mother. He embraces her.*

Eilif   I missed you! Where's everybody else?

Mother Courage *stays in his embrace.*

Mother Courage   Everyone's fine, stout as trout in a brook. Swiss Cheese is paymaster for the Second Regiment; that keeps him away from fighting, even if I couldn't keep him out of the army.

Eilif   How are your feet?

Mother Courage   Too swollen for shoes in the morning.

The **General** *has joined them.*

The General   So you're his mother! Got any more sons like this one?

Eilif   That's what my luck's like. You happen to be sitting in the kitchen so you can hear your son called a hero.

Mother Courage   You're goddamned right I heard.

She slaps **Eilif**.

Eilif (*holding his cheek*)   For taking the oxen?

Mother Courage   For not surrendering! Four peasants!? Are you nuts?! I taught you always to watch out for yourself! You brazen sticky-fingered fork-tongued son of a Finn!

The **General** *and the* **Chaplain** *laugh.*

Three

THREE YEARS LATER, MOTHER COURAGE AND THE REMNANTS OF THE SECOND FINNISH REGIMENT, STILL IN POLAND, ARE MADE PRISONERS OF WAR. HER DAUGHTER IS SAVED, AND ALSO HER WAGON, BUT HER HONEST SON DIES.

The army camp.

Afternoon. The regimental flag hangs from a flagpole. A clothes line stretches from **Mother Courage**'s *wagon to the pole, and a variety of merchandise is hanging from it. Near the wagon is a large cannon, on which laundry has been draped for drying.* **Mother Courage** *is simultaneously folding clothes that have dried with* **Kattrin** *and negotiating the purchase of a sack of bullets with a* **Quartermaster**. **Swiss Cheese**, *in his paymaster's uniform, is watching all this.*

Yvette Pottier, *a pretty woman, sits nearby drinking brandy and sewing vivid things to her hat. She's in her stocking feet, her red high-heeled shoes lying nearby.*

The Quartermaster   Two guilders. That's cheap for bullets, but I need money now, the Colonel's been on a two-day bender, celebrating with his staff, they drank us dry and where am I supposed to get money for more liquor?

Mother Courage   Not from me. That's official ammunition, they catch me holding a bag of that, I'll be court-martialled and shot. You crooks sell the soldiers' ammo out from under them, in the thick of battle what're they supposed to do? Throw rocks?

The Quartermaster   What am I supposed to do when he wants his wine, serve rainwater?

Mother Courage   It's immoral. I don't want army ammunition. Not for two guilders.

The Quartermaster   Two little guilders, come on, buy them from me then sell them to the Fourth Regiment's quartermaster, the Fourth's clean out of bullets, he'll give you five guilders for them, eight guilders if you make him out a receipt says he paid twelve guilders, and one hand washes the other and who isn't happy?

Mother Courage   Go to the Fourth's quartermaster on your own, why do you need me?

The Quartermaster   I don't trust him and he doesn't trust me, we've been friends for years.

Mother Courage   Give.

She takes the sack and gives it to **Kattrin**.

Mother Courage (*to* **Kattrin**)   Stow this in the back and give the man one and a half guilders.

The **Quartermaster** *starts to complain; she stops him.*

Mother Courage   No more discussion.

Kattrin *drags the sack behind the wagon. The* **Quartermaster** *follows her.*

Mother Courage (*to* **Swiss Cheese**)   Here's your woolens, look after them, it's October and frosty soon, at any rate it should be, who knows, you can't expect anything with any certainty, not even fall following summer. Only one thing must be as must be: and that's your regimental cash box, whatever else is awry, you keep their cash pin-tidy. Is it pin-tidy?

Swiss Cheese   Yes, Mama.

Mother Courage   They made you paymaster because you're honest, you're not brave like your brother, they like it that you're too feeble-minded to get your mind around the idea of stealing it. Which puts my mind at ease. Cash in the cash box and where do the woolies go?

Swiss Cheese   Under my mattress, Mama, except when I'm wearing 'em.

He starts to go.

The Quartermaster   Wait for me, paymaster, I'll go with you.

Mother Courage   Don't teach him your tricks.

The **Quartermaster** *walks off with* **Swiss Cheese**. **Yvette**
waves to the **Quartermaster** *as he leaves. He doesn't wave back.*

Yvette   Whatever happened to 'So long, nice to meet you'?

Mother Courage (*to* **Yvette**)   I don't want my Swiss
Cheese consorting with people like him, I don't even like to
see them walking together, it makes me worry, though in
general everything's OK, the war's going well, every other day
fresh countries are joining in, it'll last four or five years easily.
Thinking ahead and no impulsive moves, I can build a good
business. And you, with your disease, don't you know you
should lay off the booze?

Yvette   What disease, it's a lie, who says so?

Mother Courage   Everybody does.

Yvette   Everybody lies. I'm panicked, Mother Courage,
customers avoid me like the plague, it's like I hung a sign over
my cootch saying 'Remember you must die.' Why the hell am
I stitching new crap to this fucking hat?

She throws it to the ground.

I never used to drink in the morning, it gives you crow's feet,
but so what? Pride isn't for people like us. If you can't learn to
eat shit and like it, down you go.

Mother Courage   Here it comes, the why-oh-why and
woe-is-me, your Piping Pieter and how he done you dirt. Just
don't start your filthy yowling where my innocent daughter
can hear you.

Yvette   Let her listen, she should learn what it's like to lose
a man and spend ten bad years looking everywhere for him,
never finding him, she should learn what love is.

Mother Courage   That's something they never learn.

Yvette   Then I'll talk just for the relief of talking, I need
some relief. It started in Flanders because I was a girl there,
if I'd been a girl someplace else I wouldn't have seen him that

day, Dutch, blond and thin, and now I'm in Poland just because he cooked for the army, a thin cook. What I didn't know then, Kattrin, is stay away from the thin boys, and also I didn't know he had another girlfriend or that they called him Piping Pieter because even when he did it, he kept his pipe in his mouth, with him doing it was just a casual thing.

Yvette *sings 'The Song of Fraternisation'.*

Yvette (*singing*)
  We hated the soldiers,
  Their army took our town.
  I was sixteen. The foreign occupier
  Grinned as he loosened my nightgown.
      May mornings are so bright.
      But comes the dark May night . . .
      The Captain shouts 'You're all dismissed!'
      Then boys with mischief in their eyes
      Will find the girls who fraternise.
      How could I hate him when we kissed?

  The foreign occupation
  Brought sorrows – and a cook!
  By day I would despise him, then when night fell,
  I loved the liberties that he took!

      May mornings are so bright.
      But comes the dark May night . . .
      The Captain shouts 'Boys, hit the hay!'
      But one with something on his mind
      Knows just the kind of girl to find.
      We fraternised till day.

  My oppressor and my lover
  For me were one and the same.
  Everyone said, 'Her love's just convenient.'
  What we agreed on was my shame.
      A cloud that hid the sun
      Announced my joy was done.
      You have your fun but troops move on.
      You wait all night. Where can he be?

Your lover and your enemy?
His army's marching, and he's . . . gone.

She stumbles back behind the wagon. As she goes:

Mother Courage   Your hat.

Yvette   Anyone wants it, be my guest.

She goes behind the wagon.

Mother Courage   You heard, Kattrin? Don't start up with soldiers. He tells you he wants to kiss the ground over which your delicate feet have trod – and did you wash your delicate feet yesterday, as long as we're talking about feet – and bang, you're his goat cow mule and whatever else he's itching after. Be happy you're a mute, when you've finally got a husband you'll never contradict yourself or bite your tongue because you told the truth, it's a blessing from God, being dumb. And here comes the General's cook, what brought him?

The **Cook** *and the* **Chaplain** *enter.*

The Chaplain   I bring a message from your son, Eilif, – and the cook wanted to accompany me, you've made an impression.

The Cook   I accompanied you for the exercise and air.

Mother Courage   Air's free so breathe all you want, just mind your manners, and if you forget, I'm ready for you. (*To the* **Chaplain**.) So what's Eilif want? I have no extra money.

The Chaplain   Truth to be told the message is for his brother, Mr Paymaster.

Mother Courage   He isn't his brother's paymaster. And he's gone, so he can't get led into temptation by bright ideas.

She takes money from her money belt and hands it to the **Chaplain**.

Mother Courage   Give this to him, it's a sin, calculating on maternal instinct and he should be ashamed of himself.

The Cook   His regiment's marching out, who knows, maybe off to die. Add a little to that pittance, lady, or later on you'll

regret. You women come on hard, but later on, you regret.
A guy pleads for a glass of brandy, but you're not feeling
generous, so the brandy isn't flowing, and he goes off dry,
next thing he's dead under the green green ground in some
place far away and, oh, you wish you could serve him that
brandy now, but forget it, he's gone where you'll never claw
him up.

The Chaplain   Any soldier who falls in a religious war will
go straight to heaven, where he can have all the brandy he
wants.

The Cook   Point taken, though still the woman who turns
him away without a little brandy to burn his belly should burn
with shame, and not because he's a holy kind of soldier – she
shouldn't turn him away unrefreshed even if he was just your
normal undistinguished infidel infantryman off to meet St
Peter with all his venality, shooting and looting, and don't
forget a rape here and there, completely unexculpated by
virtue of his having done all those things but in the service of
his Protestant faith. Thirsty's thirsty is my point.

The Chaplain (*to* **Mother Courage**, *indicating the* **Cook**)
I didn't want him to come with me but he says he's dreaming
about you.

The Cook (*lighting his pipe*)   Brandy poured by a slender
hand, nothing contemptible on my mind.

Mother Courage   Who'd say no to a drink?

The Chaplain   Temptation! shrieked the Bishop, and fell.
(*Looking at* **Kattrin**.) And who is this comely young lady?

Mother Courage   She isn't comely, she's stay-at-homely,
and I don't want clergy sniffing up my daughter.

The Cook   Keep a gimlet eye on this dirty dog, you oughta
hear his jokes! Revolting!

The **Chaplain** *and the* **Cook** *go behind the wagon with* **Mother
Courage**. **Kattrin** *watches them leave, then she leaves her washing
and goes to* **Yvette**'s *hat. She puts it on, then sits and puts on the red*

shoes. From behind the wagon **Mother Courage** *is heard talking politics with the* **Chaplain** *and the* **Cook**.

Mother Courage   What's the news from the front?

The Cook   Nobody knows where that is.

Mother Courage   It's a mess. It was a nice peaceful invasion, the Swedish king rolled in with his troops and horses and wagons, waving the Protestant flag, he rolled here, he rolled there, he's ready to roll back to Sweden and now, now the Poles break the peace and look, blood's poured down on their heads.

The Cook   The way I see it is, I knew you'd serve exquisite brandy, I never misread a face.

The Chaplain   All our King ever wanted was to set Poland free from the tyranny of the Pope and his crony the Kaiser.

In front of the wagon, **Kattrin**, *checking to make sure she's not being seen, wearing the hat and shoes, begins imitating* **Yvette***'s provocative walk. As she continues she abandons the imitation; she becomes more confident, more mature, a pretty young woman. She even dances a little. The talk behind the wagon is continuous.*

The Cook   Absolutely. Liberty! Everybody craves liberty, the human body needs it like it needs water or bread or salt. Who knows why we need liberty? What humans need is a mystery. Who knows why we need salt? We need what we need.

The Chaplain   Amen.

The Cook   But it's expensive, liberty, especially when you start exporting it to other countries, so the King has to levy a tax on salt back home in Sweden, so his own subjects are free but they can't afford salt, or, well, the poor can't afford it, the rich can afford anything, even when it's taxed and pricey, and even better, the rich get tax exemptions!

The Chaplain   You shouldn't mock liberty. It's –

The Cook   Who's mocking?

Mother Courage   He isn't mocking anything, he's a cook, cooks have an intellectual bent, not like preachers.

The Cook   I'm talking about the human body.

Mother Courage   Right.

The Cook   A lovely thing, the human body.

The Chaplain   Created in God's image.

The Cook   You bet. Given half a chance, it'll do a little jig. It's stubborn, though. The body. Or is that the soul? Preacher? I get confused.

The Chaplain   I'm sure you do.

The Cook   It's the wanting that makes 'em stubborn, is my point. So sometimes you have to torture the people – which by the way adds to the cost of the war, since contrary to expectations the Poles have preferred to remain unliberated, the King's tried everything, the rack and the screw and prisons are expensive, and when the King discovered they didn't want to be free, even after torture, he stopped having any fun. But God told our King to fight, He didn't say it'd be fun, and it isn't much fun, is it, though since I cook for the General I have table salt at least, and the rest of it's beyond me, what bodies want and what bodies get, and it's a good thing the King's got God going for him. Or else people might suspect that he's just in it for what he can take out of it. But he's always had his principles, our King, and with his clear conscience he doesn't get depressed.

Mother Courage   Long live Gustavus Adolphus, the Hero-King. About whom a certain kind of talk is unhealthy.

The Chaplain (*to the* **Cook**)   You eat his bread.

The Cook   I don't eat it, I bake it.

Mother Courage   The King will never be defeated, and why, his people believe in him, and why? Precisely because everyone knows he's in the war to make a profit. If he wasn't, little people like me would smell disaster in the war and steer away from it. If it's business, it makes sense.

The Cook   Here's to the little people like you.

The Chaplain   Hey, Dutchman, it would be advisable to cast a glance at the Swedish flag that's flying overhead before sharing your opinions so liberally.

Mother Courage   No harm done. Nobody here but us Protestants! Alley-oop!

They toast and drink, we hear the clink of their glasses. Suddenly cannon thunder and rifle shots are heard. **Mother Courage**, *the* **Cook** *and the* **Chaplain** *rush around from behind the wagon, the* **Cook** *and* **Chaplain** *with brandy glasses in hand.*

Mother Courage   What's happened?

The **Quartermaster** *and a* **Soldier** *rush in and begin to wheel the cannon away, clothes hanging all over it.*

Mother Courage   I have to take the laundry down first, you idiots.

She scrambles to retrieve her laundry.

The Quartermaster   The Catholics! Attacking! There wasn't any warning, I don't know if we have time to –

An increase in the sound of fighting, drums and alarms.

(*To the soldier.*) Do something about the cannon!

The **Quartermaster** *runs away. The* **Soldier** *tries with all his might to move the cannon, which won't budge.*

The Cook   Better get back to my General, if they haven't shot him he'll be screaming for dinner. Look for me, Courage, I'll be back for more political debate.

He starts to leave.

Mother Courage   You're leaving your pipe!

The Cook (*exiting*)   Keep it for me, I'll need it.

Mother Courage   Of course, just when we're starting to clear a profit the sky falls in.

The Chaplain   I'll be making tracks myself, if the enemy breaks through there's apt to be serious trouble. Blessed are the peaceable, that's my battle cry. I need a big cloak for camouflage.

Mother Courage   I'm not lending cloaks or anything else, not if it costs your life. I've gone that route before.

The Chaplain   But my religious calling puts me in particular jeopardy.

She hands him a cloak.

Mother Courage   This rubs against my better impulses. Now get lost.

The Chaplain   Many thanks, it's big-hearted of you, but on further consideration it might be better to settle here for a bit.

Mother Courage (*turning to the* **Soldier** *struggling with the cannon*)   Drop it you donkey, who's paying you to do that? I'll watch it for you, it's not worth your life.

The Soldier (*running away*)   You can tell them I tried!

Mother Courage   I'll swear on the Bible.

She sees her daughter with **Yvette***'s hat.*

Mother Courage   What're you doing in that hooker's hat? Take that off, are you cracked? Now, with the enemy coming?

She tears the hat off **Kattrin***'s head.*

Mother Courage   You want them stumbling across you and making you their whore? And you've put on the shoes too, haven't you, you scarlet Babylonian?! Take 'em off, now now now!

Courage tries to yank the shoes off **Kattrin***'s feet. Then she turns to the* **Chaplain**.

Mother Courage   Jesus, help me, Pastor, get her shoes off. I'll be back in a minute.

She runs to the wagon. **Yvette** *comes in, powdering herself.*

Yvette   Is it the Catholics? Oh please God let it be the
Catholics! Where's my hat? (*She sees the hat on the ground.*) Who
stomped on it? I can't run around in that, not if it's Catholics,
they're finnicky about costumes. I gotta get to a mirror. And
where are the shoes?

She looks around for them, not seeing them, because **Kattrin** *has hidden
her feet under her skirt.*

Yvette   They were here when I left them. I'll have to walk
back to my tent barefoot. It's mortifying. (*To the* **Chaplain**.)
What do you think? Too heavy with the make-up?

The Chaplain   You're perfect.

Yvette *leaves.* **Swiss Cheese** *runs in, carrying a metal cash box.*
Mother Courage *comes out of the wagon, her hands full of soot.*

Mother Courage (*to* **Kattrin**)   Here. Soot. For you. (*To*
Swiss Cheese.) What're you lugging there?

Swiss Cheese   It's the regimental cash box.

Mother Courage   Get rid of that! You're not the paymaster
any more.

Swiss Cheese   I am. It's my responsibility.

He goes behind the wagon.

Mother Courage (*to the* **Chaplain**)   Take off your clerical
get-up, Pastor, they'll see it under the cloak.

She rubs soot all over **Kattrin**'s *face.*

Mother Courage   Hold still! A little filth, a little bit safer.
What a disaster! Bet the sentries guarding the camp got drunk.
Hide your light under a bushel, just like they say. A soldier
sees a girl with a clean face, watch out! When he's done
raping her, he calls for his buddies. (*Looking at* **Kattrin**'s *face.*)
That oughta do it. Let me look. Not bad. Like you've been
rolling in shit. Don't shiver. Now nothing will happen to you.
(*To* **Swiss Cheese**.) Where'd you leave the cash box?

Swiss Cheese   I figured it should go in the wagon.

Mother Courage (*horrified*)   In my wagon? Of all the godforsaken blockheadedness. If I don't watch every second! They'll hang us, all three of us!

Swiss Cheese   Then I'll put it someplace else, or I could take it and run away.

Mother Courage   Stay here, too late for that.

*The **Chaplain**, changing his clothes, notices the regimental flag.*

The Chaplain   Oh my goodness, the flag!

Mother Courage *takes down the flag.*

Mother Courage   Holy crap! Blinded by habit! I've flown it for twenty-five years.

The cannons' thunder gets louder.

Mid-morning, three days later. The cannon that had been next to the wagon is gone. **Mother Courage**, **Kattrin**, **Swiss Cheese** *and the* **Chaplain**, *nervous, burdened, eating together.*

Swiss Cheese   It's three days now and I'm wasting time sitting around and the Sergeant, who was always nice to me even when I made mistakes, has finally got to be asking himself: where's that Swiss Cheese gone with the regimental cash box?

Mother Courage   Just be glad they haven't come sniffing around here.

The Chaplain   Amen. Unobjectionable is our only hope. He whose heart is full of woe must sing out loud, as they say, but God and all the apostles forfend I should start singing now! I don't know any Latin hymns.

Mother Courage   One's got his cash box and the other's got an ecclesiastical sense of humour and I'm stuck between the two and I don't know which is worse.

The Chaplain   Even now God's watching over us.

Mother Courage   Which explains why I'm not sleeping well. God and your cash box keep me awake. I think I've

straightened my own position out. I told them I was a good
Catholic and adamantly opposed to Satan, I'd seen him,
Satan, he's a Swede with ram's horns. I stopped to ask if they
knew where I could buy votive candles. I've got that churchy
talk down pat. I know they knew I was lying but they don't
have any commissary wagons, so they squint a little. It could
still work out well for us. We're prisoners, but so are head lice.

The Chaplain   It's good milk. Albeit available only in small
quantities, we may have to curb our Swedish appetites. Since
we're defeated.

Mother Courage   Victory, defeat, depends on your
perspective. Defeat is frequently profitable for underdogs.
Honour's lost, but what's that? What works out best for us is
what they call paralysis, a shot here, a shot there, one step
forward, one back, and troops going no place needing
provisions. (*To* **Swiss Cheese**.) Eat!

Swiss Cheese   I don't want to eat. How's the Sergeant
going to pay the soldiers?

Mother Courage   They're retreating, they don't get paid
when they're retreating.

Swiss Cheese   If they don't get paid to do it they shouldn't
retreat.

Mother Courage   Swiss Cheese, your conscientiousness
is terrifying. Since you're stupid I decided to raise you to be
honest but really it's getting out of hand. Now I'm taking the
Chaplain to buy a Catholic flag and some meat. Nobody
noses out good meat like the Chaplain, when there's good
meat anywhere in the area you can tell because there are little
spit bubbles in the corners of his mouth and his lips get shiny.
Everything's going to be all right as long as they let me do
business. Protestant pants cover your ass same as any other.

The Chaplain   Martin Luther met a priest who was
begging for alms by the side of the road. Luther said to the
beggar priest, 'After I turn the world inside out we won't need
priests!' 'Maybe not,' said the priest, 'but you'll still need
beggars,' and he went on his way.

Mother Courage *has gone into the wagon.*

The Chaplain   That cash box is weighing on her. Everyone thinks we all belong to the wagon, but how long before they come to investigate?

Swiss Cheese   I can take it someplace else.

The Chaplain   That could mean trouble for us all if they catch you doing it. They've got spies everywhere. Yesterday morning I was relieving myself in an open-air latrine. I'd just started to squat when a spy jumped up! Right out of the latrine!

Swiss Cheese   He was in the latrine?

The Chaplain   Yes! *In* the latrine!

Swiss Cheese   Why was he in the latrine?

The Chaplain   Sniffing out Protestants! Probably sleeps down there. This one was a little stump of a man with a patch over his eye. I screamed and almost ejaculated a prayer, in Swedish, which would have been the end of me.

Mother Courage *climbs down from the wagon with a basket.*

Mother Courage   And what have I found, you shameless nothing? (*In triumph she holds up the red shoes.*) Yvette's red shoes! She's a cold-blooded thief! (*To the* **Chaplain**.) You led her straight into this, telling her she was comely! (*Putting the shoes in her basket.*) I'm returning them. Stealing Yvette's shoes! She does what she does to make a living, I understand that. But you'll give it for nothing, hoping for a little fun. But until peace comes you have no business having hopes, you hear me? None!

The Chaplain   Everyone's entitled to have hopes.

Mother Courage   Not her! I'm her mother, not you! Let her be like a stone in Darlarna. One grey stone among many grey stones as far as the eye can see, and all silent, that's how I want it with her. That way nothing ever happens to her. (*To* **Swiss Cheese**.) Listen up you, leave that cash box right where it is. And keep a close eye on your sister, she needs watching. Raising kids! It'd be easier turning weasels into house pets.

She leaves with the **Chaplain. Kattrin** *clears the dishes from their meal.*

Swiss Cheese   Not many days left when people can sit out in the sun in their shirtsleeves.

Kattrin *points to a tree.*

Swiss Cheese   That's what I mean, the leaves turned yellow.

Kattrin *gestures to ask him if he wants something to drink.*

Swiss Cheese   I won't drink. I have to think.

Pause.

She said she isn't sleeping. I should take the cash box someplace else, I found a secret place for it. All right, now I will have a drink.

Kattrin *goes behind the wagon.*

Swiss Cheese   There are mole rills down by the river, I'll stick it down into one, then I'll fetch it back. Maybe tonight just before morning and I'll take it to the regiment. It's been three days, how far have they retreated? The Sergeant's eyes are going to bug out of his head. 'Swiss Cheese, I am pleasantly disappointed,' is what he's going to say. 'I trusted you would take care of the regimental cash box and you did.'

Kattrin *is coming from behind the wagon with a glass of brandy when she runs into two men suddenly standing there. One is a* **Sergeant**, *and the other, bowing, sweeps the ground before him with his hat. He wears an eyepatch over one eye.*

The One with the Eyepatch   Nominy dominy, pretty girlie. Seen anyone around here from the HQ of the Second Finnish Regiment?

Kattrin, *badly frightened, runs to* **Swiss Cheese** *at the front of the wagon, spilling brandy, making gestures, including something about an* *eyepatch. The two men look at one another and, after seeing* **Swiss Cheese***, they disappear.*

Swiss Cheese (*startled out of a reverie*)   You spilled half of it. Why are you being silly? Did you stab yourself in the eye? I don't understand. I have to go someplace else, I decided, that's what I have to do.

He stands to leave. She frantically tries to explain the danger to him, to stop him. He gets around her.

Swiss Cheese   I wish I knew what you mean. It's something important, you poor mutt, you just can't explain what. Don't worry about the brandy, I'm sure I'll have lots of chances to drink brandy, a little spilt brandy, so what?

He goes into the wagon and returns with the cash box, which he stuffs under his jacket. **Kattrin** *grabs him.*

Swiss Cheese   I'll be back in two shakes. Don't hold on to me, or else I'll have to pinch you. Probably you mean something important. I wish you could talk.

He kisses her and pulls himself away. He leaves. **Kattrin** *runs back and forth, gesticulating frantically, grunting, trying to make words. The* **Chaplain** *and* **Mother Courage** *return.* **Kattrin** *storms around her mother.*

Mother Courage   What then, what then? You're falling into pieces. Did somebody do something to you? Where's Swiss Cheese? (*Trying to calm her.*) One thing, and then the next thing, Kattrin, not all jumbled. Your mother understands you. The biscuit-brains took the money box? I'll twist his ears right off him! Slow down and stop all this flurry, use your hands, I hate it when you moan like a dog, what's the pastor going to think? You'll make his skin crawl. There was a one-eyed man?

The Chaplain   The one with one eye, he's a spy. They arrested Swiss Cheese?

Kattrin *nods 'yes'.*

The Chaplain   It's over.

Mother Courage *takes the Catholic flag out of her basket.*

Mother Courage   Raise the new flag!

The **Chaplain** *affixes it to the flagpole.*

The Chaplain (*bitterly*)   Good Catholics now, root and branches.

Voices are heard. The two men drag in **Swiss Cheese**.

Swiss Cheese   Let me go, I'm not carrying anything. Stop yanking on my shoulder, I didn't do anything wrong.

The Sergeant   He came from here. You know each other.

Mother Courage   We do? From where?

Swiss Cheese   I don't know them. Who knows who they are? I don't know anything about them. I bought my lunch from them, ten hellers it cost me. Maybe you saw me sitting here, too salty to boot.

The Sergeant   Who are you, huh?

Mother Courage   Ordinary people. It's just like he said, he bought lunch. For him it was oversalted.

The Sergeant   You want me to believe you don't know each other?

Mother Courage   Why should I know him? I don't know everyone. I don't ask names or if someone's a heathen; if you pay up, you're not a heathen. (*To* **Swiss Cheese**.) Are you a heathen?

Swiss Cheese   Not at all.

The Chaplain   He was an orderly customer and he never opened his mouth, except when he ate. Then you more or less have to.

The Sergeant   And who are you?

Mother Courage   He's serves my liquor. And you're thirsty, he'll fetch you a glass of brandy, you've got to be parched and melting.

The Sergeant   No booze when we're working. (*To* **Swiss Cheese**.) You had something with you. You hid it near the river. Your shirt was all puffed out when you left here.

Mother Courage   You're sure it was him?

Swiss Cheese   Must've been somebody else. I saw a guy run away from here in a big puffy shirt. But that wasn't me.

Mother Courage   I agree with him, you're confused, that can happen. I know a good person when I see one, I'm Courage, you've probably heard of me, everybody knows me, and I'm telling you, he seems honest to me.

The Sergeant   We're after the cash box of the Second Finnish Regiment. And we know what he looks like, the guy responsible for it. We've been looking for him for two days. You're it.

Swiss Cheese   I'm not it.

The Sergeant   And if you don't hand it over you're dead, you know that. Where is it?

Mother Courage (*urgent*)   Of course he'd give it to you if he knew his life depended on it. Right here, he'd say, I have it, you're stronger than me. He's not that dumb. Do it already, you goose, the Sergeant here is trying to help you.

Swiss Cheese   If I don't have it.

The Sergeant   Let's go, then. We'll help you find it.

The two men drag **Swiss Cheese** *away.*

Mother Courage (*calling after them*)   He'd tell you. He's not that stupid. And don't wrench his shoulder like that!

She runs after them.

Evening of the same day. The **Chaplain** *and dumb* **Kattrin** *are washing glasses and polishing knives.*

The Chaplain   These traps into which one falls, they're not unfamiliar from our Devotional tales. It reminds me a little of

the Passion of our Lord and Saviour. There's a very old song
about that.

He sings the 'Song of the Hours'.

> In the first hour of the day
> Our Lord finally knows that
> Like a murderer he'll be judged by
> Heathen Pontius Pilate.
>
> Pilate shall refuse the blame
> Wash his hands in water
> Then the innocent condemned
> Sent off to the slaughter.
>
> In the third hour God's own son
> Flails and scourges flayed him
> On his head a thorny crown
> That the soldiers made him.
>
> Dressed in rags and mockery
> They beat him and deride him
> And the cross of his own death
> He'll drag along beside him.
>
> In the sixth hour, naked, cold
> On the cross they staved him
> As his blood spilled down he prayed
> For his father to save him.
>
> One thief laughed and one thief wept
> As he died beside them
> While the sun withdrew its light
> Hoping thus to hide them.
>
> Jesus screamed by hour nine
> Why does God forsake him
> In his mouth a bitter gall
> Vinegar to slake him.
>
> At last he gave up the ghost
> Mountains disassembled
> Temple veils were rent in twain
> And the whole world trembled.

Dark and sudden night time fell
The mocking crowd was scattered
Jesus's sides were torn by spears
The two thieves' bones were shattered.

Still the blood and water flows
Still their mocking laughter
Thus befell the Son of Man
And many people after.

Mother Courage *comes in, very worried, upset.*

Mother Courage   He's strung up between life and death. But the Sergeants's still open to talking. And taking. Only we can't let on that Swiss Cheese is ours, they'll say we helped him. It's just about money. But where are we going to get money? Yvette's snagged herself a colonel, maybe he's interested in getting her started selling merchandise. Where is she? She said she'd hurry.

The Chaplain   You're going to sell her the wagon?

Mother Courage   How else get the money the Sergeant's demanding?

The Chaplain   How will you make a living?

Mother Courage   That's it, isn't it?

Yvette *comes in with a decrepit* **Colonel**. *She embraces* **Mother Courage**.

Yvette   Courage, my love, long time no see! (*Whispering.*) It's a go. (*Loud again.*) This is my dear pal and business advisor, Poldi. Poldi, Courage. I hear you're looking to sell your wagon owing to exigent circumstances. It got me thinking.

Mother Courage   Pawn it, not sell it, don't trip over yourself, it's not so easy to find a good wagon in wartime. Two hundred guilders.

Yvette (*disappointed*)   Pawn? I thought it was for sale. (*To the* **Colonel**.) What's your opinion?

The Colonel   Your opinion's my opinion, honey.

Mother Courage   It's only up for pawning.

Yvette   I thought you needed the money.

Mother Courage (*decisively*)   No way around it, the wagon's our life. This is a good thing for you, Yvette, who knows when something like this'll come your way again? You front me the money and when I redeem the pawn, you pocket a tidy profit, you never made such easy money, your nice old pal there agrees with me. (*To the* **Colonel**.) I'm right, huh? What's his name? Mouldy?

Yvette   Poldi. And he thinks we should keep looking for something we can buy. Don't you, Poldi?

The Colonel   That's what I think.

Mother Courage   You keep looking then, maybe you'll find something you want, two or three weeks of looking is all it should take, just pray Poldi holds up, but you better hurry, he looks wobbly to me.

Yvette   I'm happy shopping with you, Poldi. You don't mind looking around for a few weeks, do you, so long as we're always together? There are lots of places to look.

The Colonel (*to* **Mother Courage**)   Well, baby girl, my knees go all stiff in this weather, I –

Mother Courage   I'll pay it back, quick as possible, with interest.

Yvette   I'm all confused, Poldi, *chéri*, advise me.

She takes the **Colonel** *aside.*

Yvette   We should give her the cash, let her pawn it, we'll own the wagon outright in the end, where's she gonna get two hundred guilders from to redeem it? I don't have two hundred guilders, but I can get money from that young blond lieutenant with the enormous feet. Know who I mean, Poldi? He's always waving it at me!

The Colonel   You don't need him, I told you I'd buy it for you, didn't I, baby bunny?

Yvette   Oh, but it's indecent taking money from someone you love when you aren't married to him, though if in your opinion the lieutenant is inclined to exploit a situation, I'll let you do it.

The Colonel   I insist.

Yvette   I'll find some way to pay you back.

The Colonel   I hate that lieutenant!

Yvette   I know.

She goes back to **Mother Courage**.

Yvette   My friend advises me to accept. Write out a receipt that the wagon's mine, after two weeks, and everything in it, I'll bring your two hundred guilders straight away. (*To the* **Colonel**.) Run back to the camp, I'll be right behind you, I just want to take stock so nothing'll go missing from my wagon.

She kisses the **Colonel** *and he leaves. She climbs up into the wagon.*

Yvette (*inside the wagon*)   You've got boots, but not many.

Mother Courage   Yvette, there's no time for that! You have to go talk to that Sergeant, tell him the money's coming, there's not a minute to spare.

Yvette (*inside the wagon*)   Let me just take a second count of these linen shirts.

Mother Courage *grabs hold of* **Yvette**'s *skirt and pulls her down from the wagon.*

Mother Courage   Leave it for now, jackal, or it's over for Swiss Cheese. And not a word who's making this offer. It came from your lover, swear that on God's good name, otherwise we'll all be implicated, his accomplices, we sheltered him.

Yvette   Calm down, I'll take care of it, One-Eye's meeting me behind those trees, over there.

The Chaplain   And when you make your first offer, it doesn't have to be the whole two hundred up front, start with one hundred and fifty, that's perfectly ample.

Mother Courage (*to the* **Chaplain**)   It's your money?
Please, butt out. You'll still get your soup, now go haggle
somewhere else, this is his life.

She shoos **Yvette** *on her way.*

The Chaplain   Apologies for interfering, but if you give
them the full two hundred, how are you going to live, to earn
money? With your unemployable daughter hanging around
your neck.

Mother Courage   I'm counting on that regimental cash
box, genius. When Swiss Cheese is free he'll bring it back to
us, we can take out money to cover expenses. I'll redeem the
pawn, we'll get the wagon back when we get the cashbox.
(*To* **Kattrin**.) You, polish the knives, use the pumice stone.
(*To the* **Chaplain**.) And you, leave off posing like Christ on
Mount Olive, wash the glasses, by evening we'll have fifty
suppers to serve. Thank God they're corrupt. They aren't
wolves, they're just men after money. Corruption is the human
equivalent of God's Mercy. As long as someone's on the take
you can buy lighter sentences, so even the innocent have a
shot at justice.

Yvette *enters, winded.*

Yvette   Two hundred even. I'll go get the money from my
Colonel, fast, soon it'll be too late, already he's sentenced to
die. They used the thumbscrews, he confessed that he had the
cash box. He told them when he saw he was being followed
he threw it in the river.

Mother Courage   The cash box? He threw it in the . . .

Yvette   It's gone. I'm gonna run and get the money from my
Colonel.

Mother Courage   But if the cash box is gone, how will I
get back my two hundred guilders?

Yvette   Oh, of course, damn I'm stupid, you were hoping
to take it outa that cashbox! I shoulda known you'd find an
angle. Well, give that up, you'll have to pay if you want Swiss

Cheese back, or maybe you want to forget the whole deal, and you can keep your wagon?

Mother Courage   I hadn't anticipated this. Don't panic, you'll get the wagon, it's lost, I had it seventeen years. I need more time to think, what to do, I can't do two hundred, you should've bargained them down. If I'm left without anything, any stranger who wants to can have me in a ditch. Go and tell them I can't do two hundred, I'll give them a hundred twenty guilders, the wagon's lost regardless.

Yvette   They're not going to agree. One-Eye's rushing me, he keeps looking with that one eye to see if someone's watching. He's scared. I have to offer the whole two hundred!

Mother Courage (*despairing*)   I can't! I worked thirty years. She's twenty-five and she hasn't got a husband. She's mine as well. Stop tearing at me, I know what I'm doing. Tell them a hundred twenty and that's that.

Yvette   Your choice.

She leaves. **Mother Courage**, *avoiding looking at the* **Chaplain** *or her daughter, sits and helps* **Kattrin** *with the knives.*

Mother Courage (*to the* **Chaplain**)   Don't break any glasses, they don't belong to us now. (*To* **Kattrin**.) Pay attention, you'll cut yourself. Swiss Cheese will be back, I'll pay the two hundred if that's the only way. You'll get your brother back. With eighty guilders we can provision a rucksack with goods and start over. It's same game everywhere, you want to cook, you cook with water.

The Chaplain   The Lord will steer us right, as they say.

Mother Courage   Dry them carefully.

They scour the knives, silent. Suddenly **Kattrin** *bursts into tears, hurries behind the wagon.* **Yvette** *runs in.*

Yvette   They said no deal. I warned you. One-Eye wants to drop the whole business, he says it's nearly over, in a minute we're going to hear the drums, the rifles are loaded. I went up to one hundred fifty. He didn't budge, not a flicker. I begged him to wait till I talked to you.

Mother Courage   Tell him I'll pay two hundred. Run.

Yvette *runs out. They sit in silence. The* **Chaplain** *has stopped cleaning the glasses.*

Mother Courage   Seems to me, I haggled too long.

Drums are heard in the distance. The **Chaplain** *stands and goes behind the wagon. Courage remains seated. It gets dark. The drumroll stops. Then it gets light again.* **Mother Courage** *sits, motionless.* **Yvette** *enters, ashen.*

Yvette   Look what you've done with your haggling and hanging on. He got eleven bullets, eleven bullets, it was enough. It's not worth it, worrying about the likes of you. But they don't believe he threw the cash box in the river. They suspect it's been here all along, that you were working with him. So they're bringing him here, maybe you'll give yourself away when you see him. I warn you, you don't know him, or you're all dead. Should I take Kattrin away?

Mother Courage *shakes her head 'no'.*

Mother Courage   She knows. Fetch her.

Yvette *gets* **Kattrin**, *who goes to her mother and stands beside her.* **Mother Courage** *takes her hand. Two soldiers enter with a stretcher on which something is lying, covered with a sheet. The* **Sergeant** *follows. They put the stretcher on the ground.*

The Sergeant   Here's somebody, we don't know his name. It's got to be entered in the record, everything in its place. He bought a meal from you. Look and see if you know him.

He takes the sheet away.

The Sergeant   Know him?

Mother Courage *shakes her head.*

The Sergeant   You never saw him before you served him supper?

Mother Courage *shakes her head.*

The Sergeant   Lift him up. Throw him in the pit. He's got no one who knows him.

They carry him away.

Four

MOTHER COURAGE SINGS 'THE SONG OF THE GREAT CAPITULATION'.

In front of an officer's tent. **Mother Courage** *is waiting. A* **Clerk** *looks out from inside the tent.*

The Clerk   I know you. You're the one who was hiding that Protestant paymaster. Think twice before you make any complaints.

Mother Courage   I'm making a complaint. I hid nobody, and if I just take what they did to me it'll look like I think I'm guilty of something. They cut my wagon and my entire inventory to ribbons with their sabres, and then they charged me a five thaler fine, and all for having done nothing, less than nothing.

The Clerk   Listen to what I'm telling you, it's for your own good: we don't have many merchandise wagons, so we'll let you stay in business, provided you assuage your guilty conscience by paying the necessary fines. And keep your mouth shut.

Mother Courage   I want to make a complaint.

The Clerk   Be my guest. Wait here for the Captain's convenience.

He goes back into the tent. A **Young Soldier** *enters, furious. An* **Older Soldier** *is running after him.*

The Young Soldier   By the Holy Virgin's Flowerbush where's that goddamned sonofabitch of a Captain who withheld my bonus and then spent it on his whores' bar tab? Time to pay up!

The Older Soldier   Aw Jesus, they're gonna slam you in the stocks!

The Young Soldier   Come out, you crook! I'm gonna butcher you! Refusing me my bonus after I was the only one willing to swim that river, the only one in the whole battalion, and I can't even buy a beer for myself. I'm not letting myself get fucked like this. You come outside now and let me cut your fucking head off!

The **Older Soldier** *restrains the* **Young Soldier**, *who's trying to get into the tent.*

The Older Soldier   Sweet Christ, he's gonna mess everything up for himself.

Mother Courage   They screwed him out of his bonus?

The Young Soldier   Let go of me or I'll murder you too, he's gonna get hung out to dry, it's gotta happen.

The Older Soldier   He rescued the Colonel's horse but then they didn't give the bonus like they're supposed to. He's young, he hasn't learned.

Mother Courage   Let him loose, he's not a dog, a man doesn't have to be put on a leash. A bonus is a bonus and it's perfectly reasonable to expect to be paid. Why else bother being brave?

The Young Soldier   He's drinking in there! You all shit yourselves for fear of him. I stepped up and stood out and now I get my bonus pay!

Mother Courage   Don't bark at me, son. I've got problems of my own, and anyway you should spare your big fine voice – if all you can do is whisper when the Captain comes out, he won't haul your ass to the stocks. People who shout the way you're shouting are hoarse in half an hour and so exhausted anyone can sing them to sleep.

The Young Soldier   I'm not exhausted and who could sleep this hungry? The bread's made out of acorn mash and hemp seed and now they're cutting back on that. He spent my bonus on whores and I'm starving. He's gonna pay!

Mother Courage   I get it, you're hungry. I remember last year when your general ordered you guys to march back and forth across the cornfields – I could've sold boots for ten guilders a pair if I'd had any boots to sell. He planned to be elsewhere by now, but here he is, a year later, bogged down, and there's no corn and everyone's starving. I get it, you're angry.

The Young Soldier   Stop talking to me, I don't give a shit about any of that, I won't let myself be treated unfairly.

Mother Courage   How long? How long will you refuse to be treated unfairly? An hour, two? See, never occurs to you to ask yourself that, and that's the first thing you should ask, 'cause it's no good figuring it out later, after all the skin on your back has been flayed off with the whipping you'll get for insubordination, after the whip's blistered all the skin off you and you're raw and bleeding, in chains praying for death it hurts so bad, then it's a little late to realise that maybe, on second thoughts, actually you can live with being treated unfairly.

The Young Soldier   Why am I listening to you? By the Holy Mother's Bush! CAPTAIN!

Mother Courage   I'll tell you why you're listening: I'm right and you know it, your fury's just a lightning bolt that splits the air, bright, noisy, then BANG! – all over. It was short-lived anger, when what you needed was long-burning rage, but where would you get something like that?

The Young Soldier   You're saying I don't have a right to get paid what I'm owed?

Mother Courage   Just the opposite. You have a right, but you have a short-lived anger and that'll never get you what you want. If you had long-lasting rage, I'd cheer you on. Hack the sonofabitch to death, I'm right behind you, but what if you cool down smack in the middle of it, and he doesn't get hacked up, because your hard-on's gone all of a sudden? There I am, standing there, you've slunk off and the Captain blames me.

The Older Soldier   You're right, he'll settle down, he just went a little crazy.

The Young Soldier   You'll see, I'm gonna cut his throat.

He draws his sword.

As soon as he sets his foot out here I'm gonna do it.

The **Clerk** *comes out.*

The Clerk   The Captain'll be out soon. Sit.

The **Young Soldier** *sits.*

Mother Courage   They say sit, he sits. Like I said. Sitting pretty. They know us so well, what makes us tick. Sit! And we sit. And sitting people don't make trouble.

The **Young Soldier** *starts to stand.*

Mother Courage   Better not stand up again, you won't be standing the way you did before.

He sits back down.

Mother Courage   Hope you're not embarrassed on my account, I'm not better than you, worse if anything. We had gumption. They bought it, all of it. Why kick, might hurt business. It's called the Great Capitulation.

She sings 'The Song of the Great Capitulation'.

Back when I was young, fresh as grass and innocent,
Any day, I'd fly away on butterfly wings.

(*Speaking.*) Not just a peddler's daughter, me with my good looks and my talent and my longing for a better life!

Singing.

If my soup was cold, or the meat they served me wasn't succulent,
Back it went, it's worth the wait for nicer things.

(*Speaking.*) All or nothing, next best is no good at all, everyone makes her own luck, I don't take orders from anyone.

Singing.

Birdsong up above:
Push comes to shove.
Soon you fall down from the grandstand
And join the players in the band
Who tootle out that melody:
Wait, wait and see.
And then: it's all downhill.
Your fall was God's will.
Better let it be.

But within a year, I would eat what I was served.
And I learned, you smile and take your medicine.

(*Speaking.*) Two kids hanging on my neck and the price of bread and everything it takes from you.

Singing.

I'd accepted that I only got the shit that I deserved.
On my ass, or on my knees, I took it with a grin.

(*Speaking.*) You have to learn to make deals with people, one hand washes the other one, your head's not hard enough to knock over a wall.

Singing.

Birdsong from above:
Push comes to shove.
Soon you fall down from your grandstand
And join the players in the band
Who tootle out that melody:
Wait, wait and see.
And then: it's all downhill.
Your fall was God's will.
Better let it be.

Many folk I've known planned to scale the highest peak.
Off they go, the starry sky high overhead.

(*Speaking.*) To the victor the spoils, where there's a will there's a way, at least act like you own the store.

Singing.

> Stone by stone you climb, but your efforts only leave you
>   worn and weak,
> Broken down, you barely make it back to bed.

(*Speaking.*) If the shoe fits, wear it.

Singing.

> From the God of Love:
> Push comes to shove.
> And you fall down from that grandstand
> And join the players in the band
> Who tootle out that melody:
> Wait, wait and see.
> And then: it just goes downhill.
> Who knows? It's God's will.
> Best to leave it be.

(*Speaking, to the* **Young Soldier**.) Stay here with your sword ready if your anger is great enough, because you're in the right, I know you are, but if your anger's only a flash, better to run away.

The Young Soldier   Go fuck yourself in hell.

He stumbles out, the **Older Soldier** *following him. The* **Clerk** *sticks his head out of the tent.*

The Clerk   The Captain's ready. You can make your complaint now.

Mother Courage   I've thought it over. I'm not complaining.

She leaves.

Interval.

Five

Mother Courage's *wagon has set up in a village that's been wrecked by cannon fire. Military marches sound in the distance. Two* **Soldiers** *stand at the wagon's bar, served by* **Kattrin** *and* **Mother Courage**. *One of the* **Soldiers** *has a woman's fur coat draped over his shoulders.*

Mother Courage   Why can't you pay? No money, no schnapps. If I'm hearing a victory march, the soldiers ought to have enough back pay to pay a bar tab.

Soldier   C'mon, schnapps! I was delayed and I missed the looting. The general only allowed one hour of looting, one hour for a whole city! It'd be inhuman to allow more, he said; the city must've bribed him, the treacherous fuck.

The **Chaplain** *stumbles in.*

The Chaplain   In the farmyard, they're lying there. A family. Somebody help me. I need linen.

The **Second Soldier** *goes with him.* **Kattrin**, *agitated, beseeches her mother to bring out linen.*

Mother Courage   I'm out. I sold every bandage in stock to the regiment. What should I do, tear up good officers' shirts to bandage farmers?

The Chaplain (*calling from offstage*)   I said I need linen.

Mother Courage *sits on the steps to the wagon so* **Kattrin** *can't go in.*

Mother Courage   I'm giving nothing. They'll never pay, and here's why, because they've got nothing.

The **Chaplain** *is bent over a woman he's carried from the yard.*

The Chaplain (*to the woman*) Why did you stay after the shooting started?

The Farmer's Wife (*very weak*) Farm.

Mother Courage Them let go of what's theirs? Oh no never! And I should be left holding the bill. Not me, no way.

First Soldier Too bad they wouldn't convert.

Mother Courage They would have if anyone'd asked. They'd whistle any tune you wanted. The farm's everything to farmers.

Second Soldier Anyway, not a one of them is Protestant. These are Catholics, same as us.

First Soldier That's the trouble with artillery shells, they're indiscriminate.

The **Chaplain** *has carried the* **Farmer** *from the yard.*

Farmer My arm's ripped open.

The Chaplain Where's the linen?

Everyone looks at **Mother Courage** *who doesn't move.*

Mother Courage Taxes, tolls, penalties and payoffs! I can't spare a thing.

Growling, **Kattrin** *picks up a plank and threatens her mother with it.*

Mother Courage Have you snapped your tether? You put that plank down now or I'll slap your face off you, you cramp! I'm giving nothing, no one can make me, I've got myself to think about.

The **Chaplain** *lifts her off the steps and puts her on the ground. He goes into the wagon and comes out with linen shirts, which he proceeds to tear into strips.*

Mother Courage Oh not my shirts! That's half a guilder I paid per. I'm ruined!

A baby is heard screaming in terror inside the house.

The Farmer   Baby's still inside!

Kattrin *rushes into the house. The* **Farmer's Wife** *tries to sit up, the* **Chaplain** *restrains her.*

The Chaplain (*to the* **Farmer's Wife**)   Stay, stay, they've gone in to get it.

Mother Courage   Stop her, the roof might collapse.

The Chaplain   I'm not going in there again.

Mother Courage   Leave off my poor linen, you jackass.

Kattrin *emerges from the rubble, carrying an infant.*

Mother Courage   Oh what luck, who's found herself another suckling to haul around? You give it back to its mother one-two-three before you get attached and I have to spend hours pulling it away, you hear me? (*To the* **Second Soldier**.) Stop gawping, go tell them they can stop that music, I don't need to hear about it, I can see they've had a victory. I've had only losses from your victory.

The **Chaplain** *is bandaging wounds.*

The Chaplain   This isn't stopping the bleeding.

Kattrin *rocks the baby, singing a cradle song in her thick inarticulate way.*

Mother Courage   Look at her, joy sitting in the midst of misery, now give it back, its mother's coming to.

She grabs the **First Soldier**, *who's been pouring himself drinks and is now trying to get away with the whole bottle.*

Mother Courage   Pay up, pig, no victories for you here, animal! Pay up.

First Soldier   With what?

She tears the fur coat off his shoulders.

Mother Courage   Leave me the coat, which anyway you stole somewhere.

The Chaplain   Someone's still inside.

Six

NEAR THE BAVARIAN CITY OF INGOLSTADT MOTHER
COURAGE OBSERVES THE FUNERAL OF THE FALLEN
IMPERIAL FIELD MARSHAL TILLY. DISCUSSIONS TAKE
PLACE REGARDING WAR HEROES AND THE DURATION OF
THE WAR. THE CHAPLAIN COMPLAINS THAT HE'S
WASTING HIS TALENTS, AND DUMB KATTRIN GETS THE
RED SHOES. THE YEAR'S RECORDED: 1632.

Inside a canteen tent **Mother Courage** *has set up. A bar in the back
is open to serve people outside. Rain. Drumrolls and sad music in the
distance. The* **Chaplain** *and the* **Regimental Secretary** *are
playing a board game.* **Mother Courage** *and her daughter are taking
stock.*

The Chaplain   The funeral cortege has set forth.

Mother Courage   Too bad about the Field Marshal –
twenty-two pairs of socks – he was up at the front before the
battle, inspiring yet another regiment, don't fear death and
that sort of thing, then he headed back to HQ but there was
fog on the meadows and he got turned around and ended up
in the middle of the slaughter and he caught a musket ball in
the gut – we've only got four lanterns left.

Someone outside whistles and **Mother Courage** *goes to tend the bar.*

Mother Courage   You guys are shameless, he was your
Field Marshal and you're skipping his funeral!

She serves them drinks.

The Regimental Secretary   It was a mistake, paying
them before the funeral. Now instead of attending, they're all
getting soused.

The Chaplain (*to the* **Regimental Secretary**)   Shouldn't
you be at the funeral?

The Regimental Secretary   I wanted to go but it's raining.

Mother Courage   You've got an excuse, the rain'd ruin
your uniform. They're saying they wanted to ring church bells

for the funeral, the way you ought to, but the Field Marshal blew up every steeple in Ingolstadt, so no bells for the poor bastard as his coffin's dropped down to the worms. They'll fire off the cannons, just to keep it from getting too sober – seventeen bullet belts.

Calls from outside, men at the bar:

Voices Outside   COME ON! SERVICE! BRANDY!!

Mother Courage   Show me your money first. And no one comes inside, you're not mucking up my tent with your filthy boots. You'll drink outside, rain rain go away. (*To the* **Regimental Secretary**.) Only commissioned officers get in. On a memorable occasion such as this you want classier company.

A funeral march. Everyone looks outside.

The Chaplain   They're filing past the estimable corpse.

Mother Courage   It grieves me in a special way when it's a field marshal or a king who dies, someone who dreamed of doing things that'll still be talked about ages hence, whose strivings fell flat all because big dreamers need common people to do the sweaty work, and common people have no aspirations, a cold mug of beer in some friendly saloon and they're happy. Look at those men out there, drinking brandy in the rain. It's pathetic is what it is, that tiny-mindedness.

The Chaplain   Oh, they're not so bad. Soldiers. They do what they're told. They'll fight for a hundred more years if they're ordered to. Two hundred years. Tell 'em to do it and they'll fight for ever.

Mother Courage   Think the war will end now?

The Chaplain   Why? Because a field marshal died? Don't be silly. Food's scarce, not field marshals.

Mother Courage   Seriously, for me it's not a casual question, I could really beef up the inventory, I've got cash and prices are low, but then if the war ends, no demand, I'll be sunk.

The Chaplain   Very well then, my earnest opinion. There are always people who run around and say, 'Some day the war will end.' I say no one can say whether the war will end. There will of course be brief pauses, intermissions if you will. The war might meet with an accident, same as the Field Marshal. There are risks in every enterprise, the earth is under heaven and nothing's perfect upon it. Wars get stuck in ruts, no one saw it coming, no one can think of everything, maybe there's been short-sighted planning and all at once your war's a big mess. But the Emperor or the King or the Pope reliably provides what's necessary to get it going again. This war's got no significant worries as far as I can see, a long life lies ahead of it.

A soldier is singing at the bar.

The Soldier (*singing*)
    A schnapps, landlord, and fast!
    A soldier's never last!
    His fists are even faster!

(*Speaking.*) Make mine a double, today's a holiday!

Mother Courage   I must be getting tired, or it's the rain or the funeral or something, uncertainty's never bothered me before.

The Chaplain   What's uncertain? What will ever stop the war?

The Soldier (*singing*)
    Your tits, girl, show 'em fast!
    A soldier's heart is vast!
    But please don't tell the pastor!

The Regimental Secretary (*abruptly*)   And peace, whatever happened to that? I'm from Bohemia and I want to go home.

The Chaplain   Oh, yes, peace indeed. It's the hole in the cheese, we search high and low for it after we've eaten.

The Soldier (*singing*)
    Your cards, comrades, and fast!

A soldier's not tight-assed!
He smiles at disaster!

Your prayer, good priest, and fast!
A soldier's die is cast!
He's mincemeat for his master!

The Regimental Secretary   People can't live without peace.

The Chaplain   True, but just because there's war doesn't mean there's no peace, war has its moments of peace. War satisfies every human need, even for peace, it's got to or why else would we have wars? You can take a dump in wartime exactly as you do when things are peaceful, and between one battle and the next have a beer. Even when you're dog weary on the march you can prop your head up on your elbows and catch a nap in a ditch. While it's true that in the thick of battle you can't play cards, you can't do that in the thick of peacetime either, when you're ploughing furrows in the field, hour by hour day after day – after a battle, at least, if you win, there are possibilities. Your leg's shot up, maybe, and first thing you scream, then you calm down, then a glass of schnapps, then in the end you're hopping about like a regular flea and the war's still the war, unperturbed by your misadventure. And what's to stop you from multiplying in the midst of slaughter, behind a barn or anyplace, breeding like maggots in raw meat, nothing stops that, and then the war takes the kids you produce and on and on it goes on and on and on. No, war always finds a way. Why should it ever end?

Kattrin *has stopped working. She's holding a basket full of bottles and is staring at the* **Chaplain**.

Mother Courage   OK, I'm buying more goods. On your say-so.

Kattrin *suddenly throws the basket to the ground and runs off.*

Mother Courage   Kattrin! (*Laughing.*) Jesus, she's waiting for peace. I promised her she'd get a husband when peace arrives.

Mother Courage *runs after her. The* **Regimental Secretary** *stands up.*

The Regimental Secretary   While you chattered I paid attention to the game. I win. Pay up.

Mother Courage *returns with* **Kattrin.**

Mother Courage   A little more war, a little more money, peace'll be sweeter for the wait. You go to town, ten minutes' walk, get our package at the Golden Lion, the pricey things, the rest we'll pick up with the wagon. They expect you, and the Regimental Secretary here will accompany you. Most everyone's at the Field Marshal's funeral, nothing can happen to you. Hang tight to the package, anyone says they'll help carry it no thanks, think about your trousseau.

Kattrin *covers her head with a scarf and leaves with the* **Regimental Secretary.**

The Chaplain   You think it's a good idea, letting her go with him?

Mother Courage   She should be so pretty that a man like him pays attention to her.

The Chaplain   Often I sit back and watch you, amazed. Your quick mind, your indomitable spirit, it's the right name for you, Courage.

Mother Courage   You're talkative today. I'm not courageous. Only poor people need courage. Why, because they're hopeless. To get out of bed each morning, or plough a potato field in wartime, or bring kids with no prospects into the world – to live poor, that takes courage. Consider how easily and often they murder each other, they need courage just to look one another in the face. They trudge along, uncomplainingly carrying the Emperor and his heavy throne and the Pope and his stone cathedral, they stagger, starving, bearing the whole thundering weight of the great wealth of the wealthy on their broad stupid backs, and is that courage? Must be, but it's perverted courage, because what they carry on their backs will cost them their lives.

She sits, takes a small pipe from a pocket, lights it and smokes.

You could be chopping up kindling.

*The **Chaplain** reluctantly takes off his coat, picks up a hatchet and a bundle of branches, and starts chopping kindling, standing over a chopping block, hacking the branches into smaller sticks.*

The Chaplain   I'm a pastor, not a woodcutter.

Mother Courage   I don't have a soul so I don't need a pastor. I have a stove, and it needs firewood.

The Chaplain   Where'd you get that stubby little pipe?

Mother Courage   It's a pipe, who knows?

The Chaplain   It's not a pipe, or rather not just a pipe, it's special.

Mother Courage   Is it?

The Chaplain   It's the stubby little pipe of the cook from the Oxenstjerna Regiment.

Mother Courage   If you know, why're you asking, hypocrite?

The Chaplain   Because I don't know whether you pay attention to what you smoke. Could be you just fish around in your pockets like some people do and any stumpy grubby snub of a pipe your fingers come across, you'll pop it in your mouth from sheer absent-mindedness.

Mother Courage   As long as I can suck smoke out of it, I'm not fussy.

The Chaplain   Perhaps, only I don't think so. Not you. You know what you're smoking.

Mother Courage   This is going somewhere?

The Chaplain   Listen to me, Courage. It's my obligation as your minister. It's hardly likely you'll meet up with that character again, and you know what character I mean, but that's luck not loss.

Mother Courage   Seemed nice enough to me. Who cares what you think?

The Chaplain   Good, you think he was nice, I think he wasn't, I think he's maybe not actually evil, but nice, definitely not. A Don Juan, exceedingly well-oiled. Take a look at that pipe, it exposes him, his personality.

Mother Courage   I'm looking at it.

The Chaplain   The stem of which has been half chewed through. As if a rat had attacked it. The gnawed-upon pipe of a boorish violent rat of a man, you can see it for yourself if you haven't lost your last lick of horse sense.

Mother Courage   You're really going to town with that hatchet.

The Chaplain   I'm not trained to do this, I'm trained to preach. I went to divinity school. My gifts, my abilities are squandered on physical activity. It's an inappropriate application of God-given talents. Which is sinful. You never heard me preach. I can so intoxicate a battalion they think the enemy army's a grazing flock of fine fat mutton. When I preach, a soldier's life's no more to him than an old *fershtunkeneh* footwrap he casts away as he marches off to glory. God gave me a mighty tongue. When I preach people fall dumb and go blind.

Mother Courage   Jesus, that's sort of terrifying.

The Chaplain   Courage, I've been waiting for this opportunity to talk to you.

Mother Courage   Maybe if we're quiet we'll hear more funeral music.

The Chaplain   Beneath your customarily brusque and businesslike manner you're human, a woman, you need warmth.

Mother Courage   I'm warm, and all it takes is a steady supply of chopped wood.

The Chaplain   Kindling aside, Courage, shouldn't we make our relationship a closer one? I mean, consider how the whirligig of war has whirled us two together.

Mother Courage   I think we've whirled close as we're ever going to get. I cook, you eat what I cook, you do this and that and when you feel like it you chop kindling.

The **Chaplain** *moves towards her.*

The Chaplain   You know perfectly well that when I use the word 'close' I don't mean cooking or eating or kindling.

Mother Courage   Don't come at me waving that axe.

The Chaplain   I'm not a figure of fun. You make me a figure of fun. I'm a man with his dignity and I'm tendering you a considered, legitimate proposal. I'm proposing! Respond to my proposal!

Mother Courage   Give it a rest, Pastor. We get along, don't make me dunk your head in a pail. I want nothing more than for me and my children to get through all this with our wagon. I have nothing to give anyone, and anyway there's no room inside me for private dramas. It's drama enough, stocking up with the Field Marshal fallen and everyone talking about peace. If my business folds, where would you be? Look, you hesitate, you don't know. If you make kindling we'll be warm come evening, and that's a lot, these days. (*She stands up.*) What's that?

Kattrin *enters, a large cut across her forehead and over an eye. She carries many packages, leather goods, a drum and other things as well.*

Mother Courage   What, what, did somebody attack you? On your way back? Someone attacked her on the way back! Bet it was that soldier who was getting drunk! I shouldn't have sent you. Drop those things! It's not so terrible, a bad scratch. I'll bandage you up and in a week you're healed. They're not human, none of 'em, every one of them's swine.

She bandages **Kattrin**'*s wounds.*

The Chaplain   Blame the ones who start the wars. They don't rape back home.

Mother Courage   I'll blame who I want and the hell they don't. Why didn't the Regimental Secretary walk you back?

Probably he figured an upstanding person such as yourself wouldn't get bothered by anyone. The wound's not deep, it won't leave a mark. Done and done, wrapped tight. You just rest, calm yourself. I've got a secret something to show you, you'll see.

She gets a sack from which she takes **Yvette**'s *red shoes.*

Mother Courage   All right, look! See? You've been dreaming about them. They're yours. Put them on quick, before I have second thoughts. You won't be scarred, though there are worse things than that. If you're pretty you've got to be afraid of what's hiding behind every bush, your life's a nightmare. It's the ones no one wants who manage to have a life, like with trees, the tall beautiful trees get felled for roof beams, but the crippled and crooked trees get overlooked and go on living. You have to know how to recognise good luck. The shoes are ready to be worn, I've been shining them on the sly.

Kattrin *leaves the shoes and crawls into the wagon.*

The Chaplain   Hopefully she won't be disfigured.

Mother Courage   It'll scar. Peace will never come for her.

The Chaplain   She didn't let them take your merchandise.

Mother Courage   I shouldn't have made such a fuss about that, maybe. I wish I knew what it looked like inside her head! She stayed out all night just once in all these years. After that she stumped around the way she does, only she started to work herself till she dropped, every day. She'd never tell me about it, what adventures she'd had. I clubbed my forehead with my fists for a long time over that one.

She picks up the goods **Kattrin** *dropped and angrily inspects them.*

Mother Courage   War! A great way to make a living!

Cannon fire.

The Chaplain   Now they're burying the Field Marshal. A moment in history.

Mother Courage   The only history I know is today's the day they hit my daughter in the eye. She's more than halfway to done-for now, no husband for her now, and her such a great fool for children, she's mute because of the war, that too, when she was little a soldier stuffed something in her mouth. I'll never see Swiss Cheese again, and where Eilif is only God knows. It's a curse, this fucking war.

Seven

MOTHER COURAGE AT THE HEIGHT OF HER BUSINESS CAREER.

A highway. The **Chaplain** *and* **Kattrin** *are pulling the wagon, festooned with new wares.* **Mother Courage** *walks alongside, wearing a necklace made of silver thalers.*

Mother Courage   I won't let you knock the war. Everyone says the weak are exterminated, but the weak don't fare any better in peacetime. War feeds its people better.

She sings:

It overwhelms all opposition,
it needs to grow or else it dies.
What else is war but competition,
A profit-building enterprise?

(*Speaking.*) You can't hide from it. The ones who hide are the first it finds.

War isn't nice, you hope to shirk it,
You hope you'll find someplace to hide.
But if you've courage you can work it,
And put a tidy sum aside.
The refugees? Oh sure, I've seen 'em,
the thousands fleeing from the war!
They've not a scrap of bread between 'em.
I wonder what they're running for?

The Spring has come, and Winter's dead.
The snow has gone, so draw a breath!
Let Christian souls crawl out of bed,
pull on their socks and conquer death!

They keep pulling.

Eight

IN THE SAME YEAR THE SWEDISH KING, GUSTAVUS
ADOLPHUS, FALLS IN THE BATTLE OF LÜTZEN. PEACE
THREATENS TO RUIN MOTHER COURAGE'S BUSINESS.
HER BRAVE SON DOES ONE HEROIC DEED TOO MANY
AND COMES TO AN IGNOMINIOUS END.

An army camp. A summer's morning. Outside the wagon, an **Old
Woman** *and a* **Young Man**, *her son, are waiting. The son
is carrying a heavy mattress.*

Mother Courage's Voice (*inside the wagon*)   Does it have to
be so goddamned early?

The Young Man   We've been walking all night, twenty
miles, we have to get back today.

Mother Courage's Voice (*inside the wagon*)   Who's buying
mattresses? People don't have houses.

The Young Man   Come look at it.

The Old Woman   She doesn't want it, no one does. Let's
go home.

The Young Man   Home's forfeit if we can't pay the taxes.
She'll give us at least three guilders for the bed if we include
your crucifix.

Bells start ringing.

The Young Man   Listen, Mama!.

Offstage Voices   Peace! The Swedish King is dead!

Mother Courage *sticks her head out of the wagon. Her hair's an uncombed mess.*

Mother Courage   What's with the bells? It's Wednesday!

The **Chaplain** *crawls out from under the wagon.*

The Chaplain   What's the shouting about?

Mother Courage   Don't tell me peace has broken out, I've just replenished my entire stock.

The Chaplain (*shouting to the rear*)   Is it peace?

A Voice   The war was over three weeks ago, they're saying, it took three weeks for the news to get here!

Another Voice   In town, a whole heap of Lutherans arrived in their carts, they brought the news with them.

The Young Man   Ma, it's peace!

The **Old Woman** *collapses. Her son rushes to her.*

The Young Man   Ma? MA!

Mother Courage *goes back inside the wagon.*

Mother Courage   Mary and Joseph! Kattrin, it's peace! Put your black dress on! We'll go find a Protestant church. We should pray for Swiss Cheese. I can't believe it!

The Young Man   They wouldn't be saying it if it wasn't true. They made peace. (*To his mother.*) Can you stand up?

The **Old Woman** *stands.*

The Young Man   I'll start making saddles again, I'll open up the shop. I promise you. Everything will go back to what it was. We'll bring back Daddy's bedding. Can you walk? (*To the* **Chaplain**.) It hit her hard. The news. She decided long ago the war would last for ever. (*To his mother.*) Daddy always said otherwise. Let's get home.

The mother and son leave.

Mother Courage (*inside the wagon*)   Give the old woman a schnapps!

The Chaplain   Gone. Gone.

Mother Courage (*inside the wagon*)   What're they up to in the camp?

The Chaplain   There's a huge crowd. I'll go over. Think I should put on my evangelical garb?

Mother Courage (*inside the wagon*)   If it was me, I'd inquire a little more precisely as to the state of things before I went into a Catholic army camp dressed as the Antichrist. I'm so happy it's peace, I don't care if I'm ruined. At least two of my children survived the war, I saw to that. Bet I'll see my Eilif soon.

The **Cook** *enters, haggard, carrying a bundle.*

The Chaplain   And look what peace already dragged in. It's the General's cook!

The Cook   What's this apparition I see before me? The Holy Ghost? No, it's the General's chaplain, same as ever, pale as a snail's sticky underbelly!

The Chaplain   Courage, a visitor!

Mother Courage *climbs down from the wagon.*

Mother Courage   The General's cook. After all these years.

The Cook   At the first opportunity, as promised, a visit, a little intelligent conversation, some unforgettable brandy, Mrs Fierling, a man's only as good as his word.

Mother Courage   Where's Eilif, my eldest?

The Cook   He left before I did, on his way here same as me. Funny he isn't here yet, he's so robust.

The Chaplain   I'm putting on my pastoral vestments, don't say anything interesting till I get back.

He goes behind the wagon.

Mother Courage   He's robust but he dawdles. He'll show up any minute, I can feel it! (*Calling into the wagon.*) Kattrin, Eilif's coming! Bring the cook a glass of brandy, Kattrin!

Kattrin *doesn't come out.*

Mother Courage (*calling into the wagon*)   Comb your bangs down over it, it's enough already! Mr Lamb isn't a stranger.

She gets the brandy herself.

She won't come out, what does peace mean to her? It took its time coming and it came too late. They hit her, right above the eye, you can barely see the scar now, but to her mind people stare.

The Cook   War.

They sit.

Mother Courage   You're showing up at an unlucky moment for me, Cook. Ruined. I took the Chaplain's advice and I've overstocked, forked over all my cash for goods I'll be sitting on, the troops'll be packing up and heading home.

The Cook   A woman your age listening to a preacher? For shame. I meant to warn you back when to give that dried-up-twig of a chaplain a wide berth but there wasn't time, and you – you fell for his big words.

Mother Courage   I fell for nothing. He's chief dishwasher and assistant drayhorse and that's it.

The Cook   You must be hard up for drayhorses. He tell you any of his sideways jokes, he's sort of got a careless opinion of women, I tried to use my influence for moral improvements but in vain, the man's absolutely unsolid.

Mother Courage   You're solid, huh?

The Cook   If I'm anything, I'm solid. (*Toasting her.*) *Skol!*

Mother Courage   *Prosit!*

The Cook   *A votre santé!*

Mother Courage   Mud in yer eye. I've only been with one solid man, thank God. Soon as spring arrived for a little extra pocket money he stripped the blankets from the kids' beds, then he told me my harmonica wasn't a Christian instrument.

The Cook   I like a woman who knows how to handle a harmonica.

Mother Courage   Maybe later, if the mood strikes me, I might play a snatch.

The Cook   Here we sit, together again, and the bells are chiming peace, peace peace . . . And then there's your indelible brandy, your unimpeachable hospitality.

Mother Courage   Did you get paid before you deserted?

The Cook (*hesitantly*)   Not exactly, no, they've been out of cash all year. So I didn't desert, non-payment of our salaries inspired us to dissolve our regiment on our own authority.

Mother Courage   You're broke.

The Cook   Oh really you know, they could stop that fucking din. I'm not broke, I'm between money, looking for something to which I can apply these capable hands, I've lost my appetite as it were for army cooking, they give me roots and boots for the soup pot then they throw the consequences piping hot in my face. I begged to be transferred to the infantry, and now, peacetime.

The **Chaplain** *appears in his pastor's coat.*

The Cook (*to* **Mother Courage**)   Later.

The Chaplain   Apart from the occasional moth hole, it's perfectly presentable.

The Cook   But not worth the effort, putting it on. No more soldiers to inflame. And I have another chicken to pluck with you, if you've the time, because thanks to you this lady purchased surplus goods under the illusion you peddled her that the war will go on eternally.

The Chaplain (*heatedly*)   I'm going to have to ask you how this is any concern of yours?

The Cook   It's unscrupulous, what you did! Interfering in the way other people manage their affairs with unasked-for advice.

The Chaplain   I interfered? Who says I interfered? (*To* **Mother Courage**.) Did you say I interfered?

Mother Courage   Don't get excited, the Cook's entitled to his personal opinion.

The Chaplain   I didn't know you owed him perusal of your accounts.

Mother Courage   I owe him quatsch, and I owe you quatsch, and his point is your war was a bust, and he's got a point. You ruined me.

The Chaplain   The way you talk about peace, Courage, it's a sin. You're a hyena of the battlefields.

Mother Courage   I'm what?

The Cook   He who insults my friend deals with me.

The Chaplain   I wasn't talking to you. You have transparent intentions. (*To* **Mother Courage**.) But when I see you picking up peace disdainfully betwixt your thumb and forefinger as if it were a, a, a snot-rag, my humanity's affronted; I see you as you are, a woman who hates peace and loves war, as long as you can make money off it, but don't forget the old saying, 'If you want to dine with the Devil bring a long spoon!'

Mother Courage   I didn't ask the war to linger and it didn't linger any longer than it wanted to. And anybody calls me a hyena is looking for a divorce.

The Chaplain   The whole world's finally, finally able to draw a deep breath and you alone, you, carping about peace because, because what, because of that load of tattery antiquated crap in your wagon?!

Mother Courage   My wares aren't crap, and I survived by selling them, and you survived by leeching off me.

The Chaplain   By leeching off war! My point! Right!

The Cook (*to the* **Chaplain**)   Adults should neither give nor receive advice, according to someone or other. Who probably knew what he was talking about. (*To* **Mother Courage**.) Sell quick before prices fall much farther. Dress up and get going, there isn't a second to spare!

Mother Courage   Sharp thinking. I like it, I'll do it.

The Chaplain   On his say-so?

Mother Courage   Better his than yours! Anyone asks, I'm off to the market.

She goes into the wagon.

The Cook   Score one for me, Pastor. You don't think quick on your feet. You should have said, 'When did I ever advise you? A little political hypothesising was all it was!' You're outflanked. Cockfighting doesn't suit men who're dressed like that.

The Chaplain   If you don't shut up, whether or not it suits my clothes, I'm going to murder you.

The **Cook** *takes his shoes off and unwinds the rags wrapped around his feet.*

The Cook   If the war hadn't turned you into the secular wreck I see before me, you could've found a parsonage to settle in, what with peace and all. No one needs a cook when there's no food, but folks still believe in things they can't see, nothing changes that.

The Chaplain   Mr Lamb, please, I'm asking you, don't push me out. I am a wreck, you're right, I've been brought low, humiliated, debased. But I . . . I like myself better now. Even if you handed me a nice metropolitan pulpit with a sinecure, I don't think I could preach. Washing bottles is better work than saving souls, the bottles come clean. Tell her to keep me.

Yvette *comes in, dressed in black, but bedizened, walking with a cane. She's much older, fatter, and she wears gobs of make-up. A serving man walks behind her. The* **Cook** *turns away and busies himself with something.*

Yvette   Hey hey, everyone! Is this Mother Courage's?

The Chaplain   Is, was, and always will be.

Yvette   Where's Courage? Could you please announce that she has a guest, Madame Colonel Starhemberg.

The Chaplain (*calling into the wagon*)   Madame Colonel Starhemberg wants to speak with you!

Mother Courage (*from inside*)   Be right out!

Yvette   I'm Yvette!

Mother Courage (*excited, from inside*)   Aaaaccchh! Yvette!

Yvette   Popped over to see what's up!

The **Cook**, *turns around.*

Yvette   Pieter!

The Cook   Yvette!

Yvette   Holy shit! Since when! How come you're here?

The Cook   As opposed to where?

The Chaplain   How well do you know each other?

Yvette   Too well!

She gives the **Cook** *the once-over.*

Yvette   Fat!

The Cook   You've been slimmer yourself.

Yvette   You're fat and I'm fat and how-de-do, you scalded hog. How many years has it been I've been waiting to tell you what I think of you?

The Chaplain   Many, many years, from the look of it, but if you could wait just a minute longer and start telling him when Courage is here.

Mother Courage *comes out of the wagon, hauling merchandise.*

Mother Courage   Yvette!

They embrace.

You're in mourning?

Yvette   Looks nice, huh? My husband the Colonel died a few years back.

Mother Courage   The old guy who wanted to buy you my wagon?

Yvette   No, his father!

Mother Courage   You look nice all right, not bad, not bad at all! At least somebody got something out of the war.

Yvette   Touch and go, that's how I do it, up and down and up and down and etcetera.

Mother Courage   Yeah, but you hooked a colonel and we have to hand it those colonels, they made hay.

The Chaplain (*to the* **Cook**)   Heaven forfend I offer advice, but you might want to consider getting back in your boots. (*To* **Yvette**.) Madame Colonel, you had something you were about to say about this barefoot man.

The Cook   Don't make a stink, Yvette.

Mother Courage   Yvette, let me introduce you to a friend of mine.

Yvette   No, no, let me introduce you! Courage, meet Piping Pieter.

Mother Courage (*laughing*)   Piping Pieter!

The Cook   An old nickname, forget it.

Mother Courage   Who made the girls throw their skirts over their heads!

The Cook   My name's Lamb.

Mother Courage   Look, I hung on to your pipe.

The Chaplain   Rarely took it out of her mouth.

Yvette   Fling his poxy pipe away, Courage, this is the nastiest fish ever to wash up on the Flanders shore. Every one of his fingers has brought misery to a different miserable girl.

The Cook   Years ago. A man can change.

Yvette   Stand up when a lady talks to you, poodle. God how I loved this man!

The Cook   I was the best thing ever happened to you, I helped you find your calling.

Yvette   Shut your mouth, you tragic disaster! (*To* **Mother Courage**.) After he disappeared and left me, um, broken-hearted, I found four other girls in town in a similar condition, and it was a very small town! Maybe you're thinking time and dissipation has ground down his teeth and horns, but you listen to me, be careful, there's danger in the ruins. If he's here hoping to hitch a ride on your wagon, show him the highway and bless his scabby backside with your boot!

Mother Courage (*to* **Yvette**)   You come with me to the market, I've got to unload this stuff before the prices hit bottom. You must know the whole regiment, tell me who to talk to. (*Calling into the wagon.*) Never mind church, Kattrin, I'm going to market. As soon as Eilif shows, give him something to drink.

She leaves with **Yvette**. *As they go,* **Yvette** *says:*

Yvette   It amazes me, a picked-over carcass of man like you was enough to overturn my apple cart. I've got my lucky star to thank, I got every fucking apple back, and then some! I've saved this woman from the catastrophe of your company, and that'll go down to my credit in the world to come. And now, at very long last, Piping Pieter, you can kiss my ass!

They leave.

The Chaplain   I suddenly find my tongue freed, I can sermonise again! I take as our text today: 'The mills of God grind slowly. And they grind small.'

The Cook   I never had a lucky star. It's just . . . well,
I'd hoped there might be a warm meal. I'm starving. I haven't
had food in two days. Now they're cluckling about me, and
she'll form a more-or-less completely false impression. It
discombobulates me, a woman's cold shoulder. I'll leave before
she's back.

The Chaplain   Better part of valour. Amen.

The Cook   Peace is as heavy as a millstone. I miss the
General, you know, God knows where he is, I could be basting
a fat roasted capon with mustard sauce, served with yellow
carrots.

The Chaplain   Red cabbage. Red cabbage with a capon.

The Cook   I know, I know, but he insisted on carrots.

The Chaplain   The man was an appalling ignoramus.

The Cook   You never mentioned that when you were sitting
next to him stuffing your face.

The Chaplain   I swallowed my pride.

The Cook   You swallowed more than that. Who knew we'd
long for those days?

The Chaplain   Nostalgic for the war. Peace seems less
hospitable, somehow.

The Cook   You're finished here same as me, you called her
a hyena. You – what are you staring at?

The Chaplain   I think it's Eilif.

A grim contingent of **Soldiers** *with pikes leading* **Eilif**, *whose hands
are tied. He's chalk-white.*

The Chaplain   What's happened?

Eilif   Where's my mother?

The Chaplain   In town.

Eilif   I heard she was here. They let me come to see her.

The Cook (*to the* **Soldiers**)   Where are you taking him?

A Soldier   Noplace good.

The Chaplain   What did he do?

The Soldier   He broke into a farmhouse. The wife − (*Gestures to indicate she's dead.*)

The Chaplain   You did that? How could you do that?

Eilif   Same as I've always done.

The Cook   But it's peacetime. You can't −

Eilif   Shut up. Can I sit till she comes back?

The Soldier   We don't have time for that.

The Chaplain   During the war he got medals for things like this, he was fearless, they said, brave, he was summoned to sit at the General's right hand. Couldn't we talk to your commander?

The Soldier   Why bother? Stealing some farmer's cow, that's brave?

The Cook   It was idiotic!

Eilif   If I was an idiot I'd have starved long before this, you asshole.

The Cook   So you used your brains and now they're going to cut your head off.

The Chaplain   At least let's get Kattrin.

Eilif   No! Don't! Leave her. Give me a taste of schnapps.

The Soldier   You don't have time for that, come on!

The Chaplain   What should we tell your mother?

Eilif   Tell her it wasn't different. Tell her it was the same. Or don't tell her anything.

The **Soldiers** *shove him and he starts to walk.*

The Chaplain   I'll walk with you on your hard path.

Eilif   I don't need you, black crow.

The Chaplain   You don't know what you may need.

*The **Soldiers** shove **Eilif** again and they leave. The **Chaplain** follows them.*

The Cook *(calling after the **Chaplain**)*   I have to tell her, she'll want to see him!

The Chaplain   Better not say anything. Or he was here and he'll be back, tomorrow possibly. When I get back I'll find some way to explain.

*The **Chaplain** runs off after them. The **Cook** watches them leave, shakes his head, then finally goes to the wagon. He calls in.*

The Cook   Hey! Don't you want to come out? I understand you, I think, peace comes and you crawl under the rug. Me too. It's terrifying. I was the General's cook, remember? I'm asking myself if maybe there's a scrap left over from your breakfast, just to tide me over till your mother returns? A little ham or some bread, we might have a bit of a wait.

He looks inside.

She's thrown the blanket over her head.

*In the distance, cannonfire. **Mother Courage** runs in, still carrying all her wares, out of breath.*

Mother Courage   Cook! Peace is finished! The war's been back on three whole days. I was just about to sell at a loss when I heard the news! Thank God! In town they're shooting at the Lutherans and the Lutherans are shooting back. We've got to get on our way with the wagon. Kattrin, pack! *(To the **Cook**.)* Look me in the eye. What's the matter?

The Cook   Nothing.

Mother Courage   Bullshit, it's something, something's wrong.

The Cook   War's started up, maybe that's it. And it'll probably be tomorrow evening before I get hot food in my stomach.

Mother Courage   You're lying, Cook.

The Cook   Eilif was here. He couldn't stay.

Mother Courage   He was here? Then we'll find him on the march. From now on I'm pulling right behind the soldiers, like I was official, it's safer. Did he look all right?

The Cook   As always.

Mother Courage   He's always the same as always, smart. That one the war couldn't take from me. Help me pack?

She starts packing. The **Cook** *helps.*

Mother Courage   Did he have any news? Is he still the General's favourite? Any more heroism?

The Cook (*grim*)   Yes, apparently, only recently.

Mother Courage   Tell me about it once we're under way.

Kattrin *comes out of the wagon and takes her place at the axle shaft, ready to pull.*

Mother Courage   Peace is already over, Kattrin. We're on the move again. (*To the* **Cook**.) And you?

The Cook   Find my regiment, sign up.

Mother Courage   You could do that I guess or . . . Where's his Holiness?

The Cook   He went towards town with Eilif.

Mother Courage   Come along, Lamb, for a bit. I need a helper.

The Cook   All that stuff Yvette was saying . . .

Mother Courage   Didn't do you discredit in my eyes. The opposite. I've always admired vitality; don't worry as much as I used to over the shape it chooses to take. Interested?

The Cook   I'm not saying no.

Mother Courage   The Twelfth Regiment's already headed
out. Take hold and pull. Here's a slice of bread. We'll have
to go the long way around to catch up with the Lutherans.
I might see Eilif this very night. I love him best of all. It was
a short peace. Let's get going.

Kattrin *and the* **Cook** *in harness start to pull the wagon while*
Mother Courage *sings:*

Mother Courage (*singing*)
From Ulm to Metz . . .

The Cook (*singing*)
                                    . . . from Metz to Mähren!

Mother Courage (*singing*)
The goddamned army's on its feet!
What if the land is burnt and barren?

The Cook (*singing*)
The war needs men, and men must eat!

Mother Courage (*singing*)
The war will feed you steel and fire
If you sign up for bloody deeds!
It's only blood that wars require!
So come and feed it what it needs!

Nine

THE GREAT WAR OF RELIGION HAS BEEN GOING ON
FOR SIXTEEN YEARS. OVER HALF THE INHABITANTS OF
GERMANY HAVE PERISHED. WIDESPREAD PLAGUE KILLS
THOSE THE WAR SPARES. IN ONCE FERTILE COUNTRIES,
FAMINE. WOLVES PROWL THROUGH THE BURNT-OUT
CITIES. IN THE AUTUMN OF 1634 WE MEET COURAGE
IN THE GERMAN MOUNTAINS CALLED FICHTELBIRGE, OFF
THE ROUTE OF THE SWEDISH ARMY. WINTER THIS YEAR
HAS COME EARLY AND IS SEVERE. BUSINESS IS TERRIBLE,
AND BEGGING IS ALL THAT REMAINS. THE COOK GETS A
LETTER FROM UTRECHT AND IS BID FAREWELL.

Outside a half-ruined parsonage. Grey morning in early winter. Wind is blasting. **Mother Courage** *and the* **Cook** *in ratty sheepskins, the wagon nearby.*

The Cook It's pitch black, nobody's up.

Mother Courage It's a parsonage. The bells will have to be rung and the Father's got to crawl to it. Then he'll have hot soup.

The Cook You're talking nonsense, the village was burnt to the ground.

Mother Courage Someone's living here, there was a dog barking.

The Cook If the parson's got anything, he won't give it away.

Mother Courage Maybe if we sing something.

The Cook I've had more than my share of this. (*He takes a letter from his pocket.*) A letter from Utrecht, my mother's dead from cholera, her inn belongs to me now. Read the letter if you don't believe me.

He proffers the letter, **Mother Courage** *reaches to take it, he snatches it back.*

The Cook From my aunt, the handwriting's a little primitive. But . . . there's stuff about what a wretched little bastard I always was, that's family matters, skip that, read here, the salient part.

He hands her the letter, which she takes and reads. She stops reading, looks at him.

Mother Courage Lamb, I can't take the open road any more either. Look at us begging. My whole life, I never begged before. I feel like a slaughterhouse dog, red meat for paying customers but nothing for me. I have nothing to sell any more and no one has anything to pay with. In Saxony one of those raggedy beggars offered me a parcel of precious books wrapped in greaseproof parchment, just for two eggs, and for a little

bag of salt in Würtenburg they wanted to give me their
plough. What's the use of ploughing? Nothing grows but
nettles. In Pomerania I've heard there's villagers so ravenous
they've eaten little children.

The Cook   The world's dying.

Mother Courage   Sometimes I see myself pulling that
wagon through the streets of hell, selling burning pitch. Or
making a living in purgatory, offering my wares to the
wandering souls till the last trumpet blast. If me and my
children could find a place where no one's shooting, I wouldn't
mind a few years' rest, a few years of calm.

The Cook   We could make a go of it at the inn. Give it
serious consideration, Anna. Last night I made my final
decision, I'm going to Utrecht with you or alone, today.

Mother Courage   I have to talk it over with Kattrin. It's
a little abrupt, and I'm usually averse to making big decisions
when I'm freezing and there's nothing in my belly. Kattrin!

Kattrin *climbs down from the wagon.*

Mother Courage   Kattrin, we have to talk about something.
The Cook and I want to go to Utrecht. He's inherited an inn.
You'd have a home, make acquaintances. There are many
men who'd want a competent somebody who helped run an
inn, good looks aren't everything. It's a good deal. The Cook
and I get along. I will say this about him: he tucks his head
between his shoulders and goes about his business. We'd know
where our next meal came from, and when to expect it, that'd
be a change, huh, nice? And your own bed, you'd sleep better,
right? Finally, life on the road isn't life. Look at us, you're
falling apart. Lice are eating you alive. We have to decide, all
right, Utrecht or, or we could just keep on, go where the
Swede soldiers are, the army up north. (*She gestures vaguely to
the left.*) We could go find the army again, but . . . I think we'll
go with cook, Kattrin.

The Cook   Anna, I have to talk to you alone.

Mother Courage   Go back in the wagon, Kattrin.

Kattrin *climbs back into the wagon.*

The Cook   I interrupted you because you didn't understand me. I thought I was clear but I guess I wasn't, so: you can't bring her. I think that's clear enough.

Kattrin *positions herself inside so she can listen.*

Mother Courage   What do you mean, leave Kattrin?

The Cook   Think. There's not enough room for her. It's not a big place. If we screw our hind legs to the floor we might keep it open and running, but three people, the inn can't support that. Kattrin can take over the wagon.

Mother Courage   I was thinking she'd find a husband in Utrecht.

The Cook   That's a laugh! Dumb, a scarred face, and old as she is?

Mother Courage   Don't talk so loud!

The Cook   What is, is, loud or soft. And come to think of it, there's the paying guests at the inn, who'd want to look up from supper and see that waiting to clear the table? How do you think this could work?

Mother Courage   I said shut up, I said don't talk so loud.

The Cook   Someone's lit a candle in the parsonage. Let's sing.

Mother Courage   Cook, how'd she pull that wagon on her own? She's frightened by the war. She couldn't manage. The dreams she must have! I hear her groaning nights. After battles especially. What she sees in those dreams, I can't imagine. She suffers because she pities. A few days back I found a hedgehog we'd killed, the wagon, an accident. She'd hidden it in her blanket.

The Cook   The inn's too small. (*Shouting.*) Worthy gentlemen, servants, and all who dwell within! In the hope of procuring a little leftover food, we will now give you a lecture in the form of a song, the Song of Solomon, Julius Caesar and other men

possessed of a gigantic spirit, which proved to be of little use
to them. All of this so you can see that we're decent obedient
people and we are having a hard time getting by, especially
this winter!

He sings:

> No doubt you've heard of Solomon,
> The wisest man on earth!
> He saw with perfect clarity,
> He would spit on the cursed hour of his birth
> And say that all was vanity.
> How deep and wise was Solomon!
> And see, before the night descends,
> He longed to taste oblivion!
> He started wise but as a fool he ends.
> Oh, wisdom's fine; we're glad we've none.

(*Shouting.*) All virtues are dangerous in a world like this, as our
beautiful song shows, you're better off having an easy life and
breakfast, in our opinion, hot soup. I for instance, I've got none
and I'd like some, I'm a soldier, but what use was it to me, my
bravery in all those battles, nix, nil, starvation, and if I'd stayed
home shitting myself I'd be better off. This is why:

Sings:

> Then Julius Caesar, mighty one,
> Raised high his royal rod,
> So brave he tore the world apart,
> So they voted and changed their Caesar to a God,
> Then drove a dagger through his heart.
> How loud he screamed: 'You too, my son!'
> And see, before the night descends,
> His reign had only just begun,
> So brave, but screaming out in fear he ends.
> Brave hearts are grand! We're fine with none.

(*Muttering.*) They're hiding in there, the bastards. (*Shouting.*)
Worthy gentlemen, servants and the whole household! You
aren't responding, you're sitting in there by your fire, and
maybe you're saying to yourself sure, bravery's not much

when you need a hot meal, I agree, but maybe if you were honest you wouldn't be so bad off! Maybe if you were honest someone would feed you or at least not leave you completely sober.

Let's test this proposition!

Sings:

> And Socrates, that paragon,
> Who always told the truth –
> They mixed a bitter poison drink
> Made of hemlock; they said he's done things to our youth
> And now we hate the way they think!
> His truth was a phenomenon.
> And see, before his night descends,
> No longer dazzled by the sun,
> He pays his bills and with a sip, he ends.
> Truths are lovely; we know none.

(*Shouting.*) You still don't want to give, and it's not surprising, who wants to give anyone anything? Sure, they tell us to give unto others, but what if you've got nothing to give? And the ones who give are left empty-handed, and that can't feel very good either, and that's why sacrifice is the rarest of all the virtues, because in the end it makes everyone feel like crap.

Sings:

> St Martin sang his benison,
> His pity flowereth.
> He met a man lost in the snows
> Who was freezing, so Martin shared with him his clothes.
> Of course the two men froze to death.
> The pearly gates no doubt he won!
> And see, before the night descends,
> So kind beyond comparison!
> Warm-hearted but beneath the ice he ends.
> Oh, pity's great; thank God we've none.

(*Shouting.*) And that's how it is with us! Law-abiding people, loyal to each other, we don't steal, murder or burn down houses! And like the song says, down we're going, deeper in the hole, and soup's a rare commodity, and if we were thieves and murderers we might eat! So if you've no food for us you better pray our patience holds out, because we know! It's not virtue that pays in this world, but wickedness, that's how the world is and it shouldn't be that way!

Sings:

At last our final yarn's been spun.
We ask you, gentle souls,
What use our loving heaven's been?
While you sit safe and soft within,
We stand without, with empty bowls.
God's love has left us here, undone.
And see, before the night descends
The way the meek are overrun.
Our virtues led us to our wretched ends.
And folk do better who have none.

A Voice from Above (*inside the house*)   You out there! Come inside! We'll give you some hot marrow stew.

Mother Courage   I'd choke on anything I tried to swallow now, Lamb. I can't argue with anything you've said but is it your final word? We've always had a good understanding.

The Cook   My last word. Take some time to decide.

Mother Courage   I don't need it. I'm not leaving her here.

The Cook   That's pure senselessness, but nothing I can do about it. I'm not a monster, it's a small inn. Let's go inside before there's no more soup, we'll have sung in the cold in vain.

Mother Courage   I'll get Kattrin.

The Cook   Come get it and bring it out to her. If it's three of us tramping in, they might get scared.

They go into the house. **Kattrin** *climbs down from the wagon, carrying a bundle. She looks to make sure the others have gone in. She drapes, over a wheel of the wagon where it can't be missed, one of her mother's skirts,* *and then atop the skirt, an old pair of the cook's pants. As she's leaving with her bundle,* **Mother Courage** *comes out of the house, carrying a bowl of hot soup.*

Mother Courage   Kattrin! Wait! Kattrin! Stop! What's the bundle and where are you off to? Have you turned your back on God and all his angels?

She grabs the bundle away from **Kattrin** *and opens it.*

Mother Courage   She's packed her belongings! You heard? I told him to fuck himself, with the shitty tiny tavern and Utrecht, what would we do in Utrecht? We don't know anything about innkeeping. The war's still got a great deal in store for us.

She sees the skirt and pants.

Mother Courage   You're an idiot. What do you think I'd have done, seeing that and you just gone?

Kattrin *tries to go, but* **Mother Courage** *won't let her.*

Mother Courage   Don't be so quick, it wasn't for your sake I handed him his walking papers. It's the wagon. I'm never giving up that wagon. It's mine, it's what I'm used to, it's not about you in the least. We'll go now, we'll go the opposite direction of Utrecht and find the army and leave the cook's stuff here where he'll trip over it, the stupid man.

She climbs up and then throws out a few things to lie near the trousers.

Mother Courage   There, the partnership's dissolved, and I'm not taking anyone else into the business ever. We'll both go on. The winter will be over some day, like all the other winters. Get in the harness, snow's coming.

They strap themselves into the harnesses, turn the wagon in another direction and pull it away. The **Cook** *comes out of the house. He sees his things on the ground. And stands there, dumbstruck.*

Ten

A highway. **Mother Courage** *and* **Kattrin** *are pulling the wagon. They come to a small farmhouse. Someone inside is singing.* **Mother Courage** *and* **Kattrin** *stop to listen.*

A Voice Inside (*singing*)
We've got a rosebush glowing
Within our garden wall.
When April winds come calling
They set the blossoms blowing
And petals will go falling,
All white and red the petals fall
When April winds come calling.

When wild geese go flying
Before the winter storm,
The autumn roses dying,
Our roof's in need of fixing!
Of moss and straw we're mixing
The stuff to keep the parlour warm
For when wild geese go flying.

Mother Courage *and* **Kattrin** *start to pull again.*

Eleven

The wagon, beaten up, stand forlornly alongside a farmhouse with a huge thatched roof which leans against a cliff. It's night. A **Lieutenant** *and three* **Soldiers** *in heavy armour step out of the nearby woods.*

The Lieutenant   I don't want any noise. Somebody even looks like shouting, gut 'em.

One of the **Soldiers** *knocks on the door of the house. A farm woman comes out. He covers her mouth with his hand. The other two* **Soldiers** *go into the house. They come out with the farmer and his son.* **Kattrin** *has put her head out of the wagon to see what's happening. The* **Lieutenant** *points at her.*

The Lieutenant   There's someone else.

One of the **Soldiers** *pulls* **Kattrin** *out of the wagon.*

The Lieutenant   Who else lives here?

The Farmer   That's our son.

The Farmer's Wife   She's a dumb girl.

The Farmer   Her mother's marketing in town.

The Farmer's Wife   For their provisioning business, salespeople, people are fleeing and they're hunting bargains.

The Farmer   They're migrants.

The Lieutenant   All right enough, you have to stay quiet, all of you, the first noise from any of you I'm going to tell my boys to shove bayonets through your thick stupid country-ass heads. I need one of you to show us the path into town. (*Pointing to the* **Farmer's Son**.) You.

The Farmer's Son   I don't know where the path is.

Second Soldier (*grinning*)   Doesn't know where his dick is. Fucking peasants.

The Farmer's Son   There's no path for Catholics.

The Lieutenant (*to the* **Second Soldier**)   You gonna take that from him?

The **Soldiers** *force the* **Farmer's Son** *to his knees and the* **Second Soldier** *holds a bayonet to his throat.*

The Farmer's Son   Cut my throat. I won't help you.

First Soldier (*to his comrades*)   Watch this.

The **First Soldier** *goes to the barn door and looks in.*

First Soldier   Two cows and an ox. Before the army I was a butcher's apprentice.

The Farmer's Son   Don't!

The Farmer's Wife (*crying*)   Captain, please, leave our animals alone.

The Lieutenant   Help us out or we'll eat your ox. (*Indicating the* **Farmer's Son**.) Hope you didn't raise stubborn children.

First Soldier   Wish I'd brought my bone saw. Here goes.

The Farmer's Son (*to his father*)   What do I do?

The **Farmer's Wife** *looks at her son.*

The Farmer's Son (*to the* **Soldiers**)   All right, all right. Let's go.

The Farmer's Wife   And many thanks, Captain, for not butchering them, for ever and amen.

The **Farmer** *stops his wife from continuing to thank the* **Lieutenant**.

First Soldier   It's the ox before everything, then the cows, then their kid, farm priorities.

The **Lieutenant** *and the* **Soldiers** *leave, led by the* **Farmer's Son**.

The Farmer   What're they planning? Nothing good.

The Farmer's Wife   Probably they're just scouting around –

The **Farmer** *has got a ladder and is propping it against the wall of the house.*

The Farmer's Wife   What in God's name?

The Farmer   I want to see how many. (*He climbs up to the roof.*) The woods are full of 'em. To the quarry. I can see armoured men in the clearing, and there's cannons, it's more than a regiment. God help the city and everyone in it.

The Farmer's Wife Any lights on?

The Farmer None. Everyone's sleeping. (*He climbs down.*) They'll kill everyone.

The Farmer's Wife The town sentries.

The Farmer Probably killed the men in the watchtower by the cliffs, or else we'd have heard their horns.

The Farmer's Wife If we had a few more of us . . .

The Farmer More than just us all the way up here, us and this cripple.

The Farmer's Wife What should we do then? Anything?

The Farmer Nothing.

The Farmer's Wife Even if we dared to, it's night and we couldn't run.

The Farmer They're all over the hill like ants.

The Farmer's Wife So there's no way to signal?

The Farmer Not unless you want to get killed.

The Farmer's Wife (*to* **Kattrin**) Pray, you poor dumb beast, pray. We can't stop the slaughter, but we can pray to God and maybe because you're a cripple He'll listen better.

They all kneel. **Kattrin** *kneels behind the farm couple.*

The Farmer's Wife Our Father who art in heaven, don't let them murder the people in the city, who're asleep and don't know that death's come so near, at least wake them up, Father, so they can see the spears and rifles and the siege engines and fires, the enemy in the night. (*Nodding towards* **Kattrin**.) Remember her mother, Lord, who's gone there, and remember to keep the night watchman wakeful, maybe he'll sound the alarm, and remember and protect my brother-in-law and the four kids my late sister's left him, may her soul rest, poor thing, save the four kids who never did nothing wrong.

Kattrin *groans.*

The Farmer's Wife   The little one isn't two yet, the eldest only seven.

Kattrin *stands, very upset. As the* **Farmer's Wife** *keeps praying,* **Kattrin** *moves quietly to the wagon, takes something from it, goes to the ladder and climbs to the roof.*

The Farmer's Wife   We have no defence but you, Lord. In your wisdom you saw fit to leave us helpless and now we ask you to show us mercy, save us and save our son and save our animals and the crops and the sleeping people in the town, the little children and old people especially, death's come in the night, Heavenly Father, and all your children are in dreadful need.

The Farmer   And we hope to be forgiven our sins as we try to forgive them who sin against us. Amen.

On the roof, **Kattrin** *starts banging the drum she's taken from the wagon.*

The Farmer's Wife   Jesus what is she doing?

The Farmer   Lost her wits!

The Farmer's Wife   Drag her down from there, quick!

The **Farmer** *moves towards the ladder, but* **Kattrin** *pulls it up on the roof and resumes her drumming.*

The Farmer's Wife   Oh, this is disastrous!

The Farmer   Stop that pounding, you cripple!

The Farmer's Wife   The Kaiser's whole army's going to come crashing down on us!

Kattrin *keeps drumming, looking towards the city.*

The Farmer's Wife (*to her husband*)   I warned you about letting gypsies put up here, think they care if the soldiers take our last cow?

The **Lieutenant** *and his* **Soldiers** *and the* **Farmer's Son** *run in.*

The Lieutenant   I'll fucking murder you!

The Farmer's Wife   Mr Officer sir, please, it's not us, she –

First Soldier   Jesus Christ.

Second Soldier   Fucking hell.

The Lieutenant   Where's the ladder? Where's the goddam –

The Farmer   It's on the roof, with her.

First Soldier   She – (*To the* **Second Soldier.**) Get the – get the gun, do you –

Third Soldier   You told me not to, it's heavy, you – fuck, listen to her.

The Farmer's Wife   She got up there without our noticing.

First Soldier   Hey girl, get down or we're gonna come up and get you!

Second Soldier   Yeah, get down here and suck my –

The Lieutenant (*to* **Kattrin**)   All right, all right, stay calm, stay calm, this is –

The Farmer's Wife   She's a total stranger.

The Lieutenant   Shut up! This is an order! Throw the drum down.

Kattrin *keeps drumming.*

The Lieutenant (*to the* **Farmer**)   You planned this, you're responsible, if she –

The Farmer   There's some tall pine trees they cut down in the woods.

The Lieutenant   So what?

The Farmer   I dunno, maybe if somehow we could . . . you know, we could hoist one of the tall tree trunks somehow and use one end to sort of shove her off and –

First Soldier (*to the* **Lieutenant**)   Can I try something sir?

The **Lieutenant** *nods. The* **First Soldier** *calls to* **Kattrin***:*

First Soldier   Hey! Girl! We wanna make a deal with you, friends, right?

Second Soldier   They're gonna hear that, they're bound to – kill the bitch.

Third Soldier   Should I go back and get the –

First Soldier (*to the* **Third Soldier**)   QUIET, goddamn it! (*To* **Kattrin**.) You, you listening?

Second Soldier   Hey! Hey you, listen to him, he's trying to –

First Soldier   We're friends, we . . . Get down, right, if you get down we'll take you with us, we promise we won't touch you –

Second Soldier   Who'd want to touch an ugly fucking –

First Soldier   We'll take you into town with us and you point out your mother and she won't get hurt.

Kattrin *keeps drumming. The* **Lieutenant** *shoves the* **First Soldier** *aside.*

The Lieutenant (*calling up to* **Kattrin**)   You don't believe him, you aren't stupid, you know we're not friends and anyway, who'd trust someone with a face like his? But will you believe me if I give you my word as an officer of His Majesty the Emperor's army? My sacred word?

Kattrin *drums harder.*

Third Soldier (*muttering*)   Well that was effective. Jesus Christ.

First Soldier   You better do something, sir.

Second Soldier   They're gonna hear that in town.

The Lieutenant   We've gotta –

Third Soldier   Torch the house!

The Lieutenant   Make some sort of noise!

Second Soldier   You told us not to make any noise, we –

The Lieutenant   Drown out the –

First Soldier   I thought we weren't supposed to make any –

The Lieutenant   Drown out the drumming, a, a normal noise, you goddamned imbecile, a peacetime sound, like –

The Farmer   Wood chopping!

The Lieutenant   Good, do it, start chopping!

The **Farmer** *takes up his axe and starts chopping at a log lying on the ground.*

The Lieutenant   Can't you chop any harder than that?

Kattrin *drums a little softer, distracted by the chopping sound, but then she realises what's happening and starts drumming all the harder.*

The Lieutenant (*to the* **Farmer**)   Louder dammit! (*To the* **First Soldier**.) You too! Start chopping!

The Farmer   There's just the one axe.

The Lieutenant   Torch it, torch the house.

The **Farmer** *stops chopping.*

The Farmer   They'll see the fire in town, that's a bad idea.

Kattrin, *still drumming, laughs.*

The Lieutenant   That does it, she's laughing at us. Get the gun, shoot her down, I don't care, shoot her!

Two of the **Soldiers** *run out.* **Kattrin** *drums harder.*

The Farmer's Wife   That wagon over there's all they have. Take the axe to that and she'll have to stop.

The **Lieutenant** *hands the axe to the* **Farmer's Son**.

The Lieutenant   Do it, you heard your mother, chop that wagon to splinters. (*To* **Kattrin**.) You want him to take an axe to your wagon? Then stop!

The **Lieutenant** *signals to the* **Farmer's Son**, *who hits the wagon with the axe, a few tepid blows.*

The Farmer's Wife (*screaming up to* **Kattrin**)   STOP IT
YOU DUMB COW!

As the boy hits the wagon, **Kattrin** *watches with a stricken expression,
making a few low groaning sounds. But she doesn't stop drumming.*

The Lieutenant   Where are those lazy cunts with the rifle?

First Soldier   LISTEN!

Everyone, including **Kattrin***, stops and listens. Silence.*

First Soldier   They're not hearing her in town, there'd be
alarm bells if they did.

The Lieutenant (*to* **Kattrin**)   Nobody's hearing you, it's
not working, and now you're going to get shot and killed for
nothing. One last time: throw down that drum!

The **Farmer's Son** *throws the axe down and calls out abruptly:*

The Farmer's Son   Keep drumming! They'll kill them all!
Drum! Drum! Drum!

Kattrin *resumes her drumming. The* **First Soldier** *knocks the*
Farmer's Son *to the ground and clubs him brutally, with the butt end
of his spear.* **Kattrin** *starts crying but keeps drumming.*

The Farmer's Wife   Oh God, please stop hitting him in
the back, you're killing him!

The **Soldiers** *run in with a large musket on a tripod.*

Second Soldier   The Colonel's foaming at the mouth,
Lieutenant. We're gonna get court-martialled.

The Lieutenant   Set it up! Hurry!

They set up the musket. The **Lieutenant** *calls up to* **Kattrin** *while
this is being done:*

The Lieutenant   All right this is the final warning: Stop
drumming!

Kattrin *is crying and drumming as hard as she can.*

The Lieutenant   STOP IT! STOP IT! STOP THE – (*He
turns to his* **Soldiers**.) Fire!

The **Soldiers** *fire.* **Kattrin** *is hit. She strikes the drum weakly a few more times, then collapses, slowly.*

The Lieutenant   No more noise.

From the city, a cannon's shot answers **Kattrin**'s *last drumbeat. Alarm bells and cannonfire sounding all together is heard in the distance.*

First Soldier   Listen. It worked. She did it.

Twelve

Night, nearly dawn. Trumpets and drums and fifes, an army departing.

Alongside the wagon, **Mother Courage** *sits, bent down over her daughter. The farm couple stand nearby.*

The Farmer (*angrily*)   You have to go now, lady. Only one last regiment left and then that's it. You wanna travel alone?

Mother Courage   Maybe she's sleeping.

Sings:

> *Eia popeia,*
> Who sleeps in the hay?
> The neighbour's brat's crying
> While my children play.
> The neighbour's kid's shabby
> But my kids look nice,
> With shirts like the angels wear
> In paradise.
>
> Neighbour can't feed 'em
> But mine shall have cake,
> The sweetest and choicest
> The baker can bake.
>
> *Eia popeia,*
> I see your eyes close.
> One kid lies in Poland.
> The other – well, who knows?

(*Speaking.*) You should never have told her about your brother-in-law's children.

The Farmer   You had to go to town to hunt for bargains, maybe if you'd been here none of this would have happened.

Mother Courage   Now she's sleeping.

The Farmer's Wife   She isn't sleeping, stop saying that and look, she's gone.

The Farmer   And you have to go too. There are wolves around here, and people who're worse than the wolves.

Mother Courage   Yes.

She goes to the wagon and brings out a sheet.

> Like simplicios Book
> +wolves represent to
> bad people

The Farmer's Wife   Do you have anyone left? Anyone you could go to?

Mother Courage   One left. Eilif.

She uses the sheet to wrap **Kattrin***'s body.*

The Farmer   You've got to go find him then. We'll take care of her, she'll have a decent burial. Don't worry.

Mother Courage   Here's money for what it costs.

She gives the **Farmer** *some money. The* **Farmer** *and his son shake her hand and carry* **Kattrin***'s body away. The* **Farmer's Wife** *follows them. She turns as she leaves and says to* **Mother Courage***:*

The Farmer's Wife   Hurry.

She leaves.

Mother Courage (*harnessing herself to the wagon*)   Hopefully I'll manage to pull the wagon alone. I bet I can do it, not much in it any more. I have to get back in business.

The fife and drums of another regiment marching by. **Soldiers** *are singing in the distance. As they sing,* **Mother Courage** *begins to pull her wagon, pursuing them.*

Soldiers (*offstage, singing*)
> Sometimes there's luck, and always worry.
> The war goes on, and perseveres!
> For war is never in a hurry,
> And it can last a thousand years.
>
> The day of wrath will come like thunder
> But who has time to make amends?
> You march in line, but never wonder
> How it began and where it ends.
>
> The Spring has come, and Winter's dead!

Mother Courage (*over the singing*)   Take me with you!

Soldiers (*singing over her, offstage*)
> The snow has gone, so draw a breath!
> Let Christian souls crawl out of bed,
> Pull on their socks and conquer death!
>
> The world will end, and time will cease!
> And while we live we buy and sell!
> And in our graves we shall find peace –
> Unless the war goes on in Hell!